It Takes Heart

It Takes Heart *By* Me

Allen *With* **Frank Graham, Jr.**

Harper & Brothers  New York

Contents

A 16-page section of photographs follows page 128.

Foreword

I met a ten-year-old boy February 2 whom I shall never forget. Bob Turley, Eddie Lopat and I flew to Binghamton to speak in the evening before some fifteen hundred sports fans at their annual Hot Stove League banquet. That afternoon the committee met us at the airport and asked if we would visit hospitalized Danny Hill. Things had not gone too well with him, we were told, what with a broken home adding to an otherwise normal youngster's natural bewilderment at life's baffling challenges. We walked in on Danny and his eager eyes lit up but not enough to conceal fully the reflections of a mind and heart trying to comprehend what had happened to him, and what might happen to him. Sports were life itself to this youngster and he lay there the victim of a train accident that severed a leg.

When they picked him up alongside the railroad tracks to rush him to the hospital Danny Hill's first words were: "Do you think I'll be able to play baseball again?"

He asked this same question as I stood by his hospital bed. This was not altogether wishful thinking. Danny was seeking a support on which to build a solid hope. I could see that he had that instinctive yearning to achieve something he held most dear. Sometimes we call that intangible quality "heart."

Danny's face brightened as I told him the stories of Monty Stratton, who lost a leg in a hunting accident and yet pitched again; of Bert Shepard, who pitched for Washington with an artificial leg; of Lou Brissie, who, after a war injury that all but took a leg, begged the doctors not to amputate because he wanted to play baseball. Miraculously they saved his limb but he was left badly crippled. Lou Brissie went on to star for the Philadelphia Athletics.

The history of the world is full of stories that tell of the remarkable accomplishments of individuals gifted with exceptional courage and spirit and unflinching desire. It is these very people who have persevered to change the course of history. But nowhere else do you find examples of heart more dramatically portrayed than in the sports world. Conquering physical shortcomings is only a part of the picture, although volumes could be written on these alone.

Joe DiMaggio is rated one of the all-time great baseball players. His skill in every imaginable department of the game was amazing, his play breathtakingly artistic. His natural talents found championship expression in a fierce pride that demanded perfection in performance. With it he was intensely selfless, a great team man, a peerless leader. He had all kinds of heart. One kind he showed in an incident I shall never forget. In 1948 the Boston Red Sox beat the Yankees on a Saturday to eliminate them from the pennant race. Boston still had a chance to tie Cleveland on Sunday, the last game of the year. Joe had a badly damaged leg that should have benched him weeks before, but with the pennant race still alive between Cleveland and Boston the Yankee Clipper withstood the pain to give his all in the interests of fair play. Bucky Harris, then the Yankee skipper, told Joe not to play Sunday. The danger of permanent injury could end his career. And now the Yankees were out of the race. But Joe insisted on playing because, as he put it, "my brother (Dom) plays for Boston and if I stayed out of the line-up some people might interpret that as trying to help his team win and be in position to tie Cleveland for the flag." Joe played, literally dragging a game leg. In the ninth inning he connected for his fourth hit of the game. At this point Harris sent in a pinch-runner and as DiMag left the bag partisan-packed Fenway Park rose to a man as if on signal and gave the Yankee Clipper as great a spontaneous ovation as a player ever received any-where. There were many times Joe had to have heart and we tell of some of them in the book.

A few weeks back while I was on assignment to televise the Rose Bowl in Pasadena former heroes of this football classic were recalled, among them an all-time All-America fullback, Ernie Nevers of Stanford. On January 1, 1925, it was Stanford versus Notre Dame—Pop Warner matching wits against Knute Rockne—the Four Horsemen and Seven Mules arrayed against Ernie Nevers and his rugged Indians. A truly memorable battle was won by Notre Dame, but individual victory went to the blond tank, Ernie Nevers, who crashed and smashed in an epic performance climaxing a season in which he had suffered two fractured ankles; he played that day with both legs so tightly bandaged the circula-tion was all but cut off.

"Heart" isn't easily defined, but it is easily understood when translated in terms of the Ernie Nevers story.

Take California center Roy Riegels, who four years later in the Rose Bowl picked up a Georgia Tech fumble on the Tech 35-yard line and in the confusion of scrambling arms and legs got headed in the wrong direction and raced toward his own goal, his own teammate helping stop him a yard short. A blocked punt followed and Georgia Tech won 8-7. Such an incident will always live, but it could easily have been

tragic to Roy Riegels throughout his life if he hadn't had the
heart to stand the gaff of ridicule and criticism through the
years to battle on to success.

Heart here might be explained in part as that quality needed
to help one overcome the faults of one's fellow men—and
oneself. Oh, how easy it is to sit in the stands and second-
guess.

Here is a man who rose and fell . . . and rose again to fame . . .
He blew a big one in the pinch—but facing jeering throngs
He came through Hell to scramble back—and prove a champ
    belongs.

These are lines from a poem written by Granny Rice. It
could easily describe Roy Riegels. It does describe all people
with stoutheartedness.

Granny was great. He had the big-league touch in all he
did, but to climb the heights he had to weather many storms
that shaped him into a universally loved member of the sports
beat. Maybe that was why he so often philosophized poetically
about the many-faceted subject of heart. Long before I ever
thought of compiling these storied examples of beating the
physical, mental and emotional odds, I stored away many of
Granny's observations.

> I've known too long the deep thrill of the race,
> The crash of bodies and the cheers that sweep
> A thousand fields, as men stand up to men,
> To prove that courage has its place again.

In the Olympic trials of 1948 Harrison Dillard in the hurdles
tripped and failed to qualify. He was the world record-
holder but an accident deprived him of competing in his
specialty. Set on making the U.S. Olympic squad somehow,
he competed in the dashes, qualified for the team, went to

the Olympics and astoundingly won the 100 metres.
Granny would say:

> To play the game out as the game may break
> Through scar and stain and dreams that go astray,
> Through fog and mist—with only this at stake—
> An unwhipped spirit through the final play.

There's the recollection of the most spectacular day any
track athlete ever had. In 1935 at a Big Ten meet in Ann
Arbor Jesse Owens shattered five world records and tied a
sixth in the dashes, low hurdles and broad jump.

But I wander away from my foreword and find my reveries
have carried me into the book itself. I meant to try and
explain "heart" and got lost among wonderful memories of
champions I've seen who have explained it more eloquently
by their deeds than I can with words.

Heart is a mosaic of man's reaction to the opportunities and
obstacles that confront him along the way to winning a reputation, with the lesson learned that its achievement is only the
beginning of endeavor, not the finish. It has been said that
from those who give much, much is expected.

Courage, mental and moral, competitive zest, pride, desire,
faith and hope, confidence and aggressiveness—these are
among the essential ingredients. But heart is difficult to pinpoint in definition because varying degrees of skill and matu-
rity can change the effect of the formula from person to person.
Heart is the spark that can make a man out of a mouse, or,
where there is greater natural ability to start with, can make
a mortal immortal.

Henry Armstrong, a remarkable champion in three divi-
sions, displayed unforgettable heart in 1938 when he sought
to wrest the lightweight title from Lou Ambers. Ahead on
points in a punch-packed thriller, Armstrong suffered a cut

inside his mouth late in the fight so severe his handlers couldn't stop the bleeding. Referee Arthur Donovan between rounds finally told Armstrong he would have to stop the fight but Armstrong begged him not to, pleaded he would stop the bleeding. He did—by swallowing his blood for the final three rounds—and fought on through painful and nauseating illness to win the title.

There are faintheartedness, lightheartedness, and then there is stoutheartedness—coming through in the clutch, if you will.

I marveled at the poise and determination of Allie Reynolds that day in 1951 after Yogi Berra had dropped a pop foul off the bat of Red Socker Ted Williams that would have ended the game and given Reynolds his second no-hit game of the year, unprecedented in the American League at that time. Seldom does one recover from giving a deadly batter like Williams a second chance. Said Allie:

"You don't dare give a hitter like Ted the same pitch twice in a row, and especially a fast ball. But I had to go with my best pitch against the best batter. And I gave it all I had."

Reynolds' heart was beating fast.

Williams fouled out to Berra.

There was the night in Brooklyn I saw young Johnny Vander Meer fight his way through a wild ninth inning to achieve a fantastic second consecutive no-hitter. His folks and friends were there to watch him pitch. With a sudden realization of what could go into the record book, he hurried his delivery and walked the bases loaded with one out. Manager Bill McKechnie went to the mound and told him he was trying too hard—trying to put too much on the ball—and was thus losing his control. Vander Meer relaxed under the tension and retired Ernie Koy and Leo Durocher for his second straight no-hitter.

In 1946 Bob Feller faced the Yankees in the last of the

ninth leading 1-0 with a no-hitter hanging in the balance. George Stirnweiss led off and reached first on an error. All Feller then had to do was retire Tommy Henrich, Joe DiMaggio and Charley Keller, one of the all-time superior outfields. Feller and DiMag battled to a full count but Bob "hung in there" as they say in the dugouts.

In sports athletes call it by the general term "that little extra." When a pitcher in deep trouble succeeds in extricating himself therefrom it is said he "reached back for that little extra," he came up with what it took to get out of the jam. It's that something extra that makes the difference. That something extra is heart.

The ballplayer who, with the bases loaded and two out in a close game, hollers to his pitcher: "Make him hit it to me, baby," that player has heart. The batter on deck who urges a teammate at bat "to get on base, I'll drive you in" is a guy who relishes closing with the foe. He's got heart who, when the chips are down, carries a bat on his shoulder.

Theodore Roosevelt said: ". . . the credit belongs to the man who is actually in the arena, whose face is marred by dust and sweat and blood . . . who knows the great enthusiasms, the great devotions and spends himself in a worthy cause . . . who in the end at best knows the triumph of high achievement and at worse fails while daring greatly, so that his place shall never be with those cold and timid souls who know neither victory nor defeat."

You will find in this book stories of athletes who are typical of the moral, mental and physical fiber of all people who make up the heartbeat of America. A blend of the will and the skill together with, in the words of Knute Rockne, "the emotional urge that lifts a man out of the commonplace." You've got to have heart.

I surely needed it to buckle down to work at the patient prodding of Evan Thomas at Harper's. It was his idea and

after a few years of unproductivity I'm sure he was sorry.
But at last Frank Graham, Jr., joined forces with me and the
deed is done. I am profoundly grateful to Frank, who follows
in his father's footsteps, and I predict will fill them well.
Patience should be the middle name of Mr. Thomas, and as
I write these words, Evan, I find the date is my birthday, and
the day rather in keeping with the title *It Takes Heart*.

MEL ALLEN

February 14, 1959
St. Valentine's Day

It Takes Heart

This is a shortened form of the famous anonymous sports-men's prayer read by Mel Allen on the evening of April 19, 1957, over the CBS network.

"Dear God, help me to be a sport in this game of life. I don't ask for any easy place. I only ask for the stuff to give one hundred per cent of what I've got. Help me to take the bad breaks as part of the game. Help me to understand that the game is full of knocks and trouble. Help me to play on the square. And finally, if I'm laid on the shelf in sickness or old age, help me to take that as part of the game too. Help me not to whimper or squeal that I had a raw deal. And at the end, I ask for no lying compliments. I'd only like to know that I've been a game guy."

Chapter 1 **Sport's Other Dimension**

Courage, at its purest, is a private matter. The great acts of heroism are chiefly those which are hidden from others, the issue of an agonizing struggle within a man as he rises above some personal trial. Performed by those who have "that within which passeth show," these acts are never celebrated in public and their reward is neither fame, glory nor money. Yet courage is a quality that has always fascinated us and we hunger for a glimpse of it under conditions which are classically dramatic. The warrior, the hunter, the mariner and the pioneer supplied the stuff of which epic tales were made in the past. Now the arena for heroism has been diminished. Science has stripped the illusion of romance from war and even partially tamed the hazardous backgrounds against which earthbound adventurers once displayed their valor. Like much else in our time, the celebrated public act of courage is no longer an adornment of the high and the mighty; it belongs to many of us.

Its appeal as a spectacle remains. It is the subject of books, movies and plays and we like to recount the courageous acts of people we have known. But to a considerable number of us the sports world serves as the most accessible contemporary stage on which men of courage, boldness and determination can be watched. The issues are defined, the performers properly identified and the whole story immediately made available to the public. Athletes are sometimes scoffed at as men playing children's games but the history of sports is filled with stories of athletes whose response to serious obstacles was not childish. Death is the occupational hazard of some. Others risk blindness, disfiguration, crippling injuries and irreparable damage to the brain. And there are the personal problems—age, poverty and physical limitations are among the most prominent —which afflict all men but whose effects can be more suddenly ruinous to the athlete. Competition among men in a sports event is a stimulating spectacle. It takes on a wider significance when one of those men is trying to overcome an adversary more formidable than his rivals on the field.

It sometimes seems that the sports world puts too heavy an emphasis on the qualities of "heart" which are said to distinguish the better athletes. Constant observation of athletes, however, confirms the theory that some of the very greatest have climbed above their rivals on guts alone. Countless thousands of healthy, strong young men compete in sports in this country and the future champion is often lost in the crowd for a time when he begins. So many things can go wrong on the way to the top that those with less heart are soon weeded out. They become the "runners whom renown outran." In the fight game the managers withhold judgment on a good-looking young fighter until he has passed the ultimate test.

"He's looked great so far," you will hear an old-timer say. "But let's see what happens when he gets knocked down."

They look for the fighter who can come off the floor to win. It is the same in all sports. Typical of the champion who will not admit he has been beaten is little Tony DeSpirito, one of the country's best jockeys. Gifted with talent, Tony rose quickly to fame. As a sixteen-year-old apprentice rider in 1952 he smashed the all-time record by riding 390 winners. The success that many men strive for year after year was his almost as soon as he had learned how to shave. And then, before he was twenty, he was struggling for his health and his career, even his life. In a bad spill at New York's Aqueduct track in 1955 he suffered a broken jaw and a lacerated brain. By January this game little guy was back in the saddle, astonishing those who had thought it might be years before he could ride again. Four months later he was nearly killed in another spill. He lingered for days in critical condition and, when he regained consciousness, he learned that one of his smashed ribs had pierced a kidney. The doctors operated and took out the rib, a kidney and his spleen. These doctors, racing officials and his friends advised him to retire from riding.

"But what would I do?" he asked, as if such a move was out of the question. "Riding is the only thing I know how to do, and it's what I want to do more than anything."

Within a year he was riding again, and riding winners. Even a slipped disc in his back and a long illness after he had returned to the track could not keep him from accepting mounts. More than that, he continued to ride as hard as he had when he was an apprentice jock, toppling records on his way to fame.

"You can't hesitate or you'll be in trouble," DeSpirito told a friend who had marveled at his bold riding in an important race. "If you don't ride all the way there isn't any sense in riding. I don't think I'm as daring as some people have said, but when I have a horse under me with enough left to move into a hole or go through on the rail, that's what I'm going to do with him. You don't win races waiting around for openings your grandmother could drive a truck through."

The athlete often has to overcome obstacles more discouraging than physical injury. The vicious slurs hurled at Jackie Robinson because of his color when he became the first Negro to play in organized baseball were far more bitter to him than the beanballs he had to dodge. Robinson's courage in those early days of his career lay in the restraint with which he conducted himself in humiliating situations. Later, when he had established himself as a great player and paved the way for the other Negroes who followed him, he threw off the wraps to vent his fury on all those with whom he disagreed. By his early will power and the spirit which made him the fiercest competitor of his time, he had earned the right to speak his piece. He made many enemies, but even his enemies admired him.

And there was Jackie Pung, the plucky woman who, at the peak of her golf career, suffered a complete nervous breakdown. Tormented by her private fears and despairing in her poverty, she battled back to win the 1957 women's National Open Championship—and then found that she had been disqualified by her partner's innocent error in computing their scores. The loss of the $1,800 prize money, which she needed so desperately, was a terrible blow in itself. Surely as bad was the loss of the prestige this title would have given her—the prop which could have bolstered her faith in herself and perhaps restored her completely to health. But the second breakdown which her friends feared she might suffer on hearing of her disqualification did not occur. In a spontaneous tribute to her courage, hundreds of golf fans contributed toward a fund for Jackie. Growing to more than $3,400, it more than replaced the prize money which many felt had been taken from her unjustly by the tournament officials.

It is ironic that the affection in which the public holds its athletic heroes is sometimes completely revealed only when misfortune strikes one of them down. Lou Gehrig, for instance, spent most of his career at Yankee Stadium in the shadow of two more widely publicized players, Babe Ruth and Joe Di-Maggio. Then, attacked by the terrible lateral sclerosis which was soon to take his life, Gehrig was the object of nationwide sympathy. Letters, telegrams and gifts poured in to him from persons he had never heard of. On Lou Gehrig Day at Yankee Stadium, July 4, 1939, the huge crowd gave a touching demonstration of its affection for the stolid first baseman. Gehrig, with halting steps, walked to the microphone which had been placed at home plate.

"With all this," he said, indicating his friends who had come there to pay him tribute and the gifts that had been lavished on him, "I consider myself the luckiest man on the face of this earth."

There was a similar response to Roy Campanella's injury. His career ended by the spinal injury he suffered when his automobile overturned, his prospects of ever walking again hanging more on his great faith in himself than on any hopeful prognosis by the doctors, Campy remained an inspiration to millions of people. And, on another level, there was the reaction of the fans in Brooklyn to the dismal batting slump which threatened to close Gil Hodges' big league career in 1952. Hodges was helpless at the plate. Those who watched him every day predicted he would never regain his batting eye. But Gil did not give up. He plodded through his personal nightmare and won the admiration of what were once the most critical fans in the world. Typical of their attitude was the concluding sentence of the sermon delivered by a Brooklyn priest to his parish:

"Go home, keep the faith, obey the Ten Commandments —and pray for Gil Hodges."

Soon Hodges was out of his slump and once more terrorizing National League pitchers. Years from now it may be that many will best remember Gil for the way he conducted himself in adversity, rather than for his many game-winning home runs. Adversity has goaded countless athletes to greatness. "If you want to see a great fighter at his best," someone has said, "watch him when he's getting licked." The crowd that saw Sugar Ray Robinson win back his middleweight championship from Randy Turpin at the Polo Grounds in 1951 can testify to that. Behind on points, raked by Turpin's punches, in danger of losing by a technical knockout because of the ugly cut Turpin had opened near his eye, Robinson was a beaten fighter. Only a supreme effort could turn the tide in his favor. Charging into Turpin in the eleventh round, Robinson called on all his wonderful skill, found the opening he needed and reduced Turpin to a defenseless target. His swift and deadly attack had snatched victory from what a moment before had been a hopeless cause. All of his greatness as a fighter had gone into that rally.

There is a point, of course, at which courage degenerates

into foolhardiness. Discretion may not be the better part of valor, but a pinch of discretion must sometimes temper it. Boxing is a sport in which an excess of courage has led to many tragedies. The sight of a man shaking off a frightful beating to come back and win is an inspiring one. The derelicts that the sport has cast aside, however, ruined in body and mind, create a sight that is appalling. Only in recent years have some of the men who rule the sport stepped in to restrain incompetent fighters from destroying themselves. Hurricane Jackson, a fighter whose mentality had never progressed beyond childhood, was the center of a dispute not long ago when he was permitted to fight in some states after the boxing commissions of others had judged him unfit. For a time Jackson was merely looked on as an eccentric young man with a passion for sopping up punishment. He had the resiliency which enabled him to shake off the punches and come back to win.

"I like to get hit," Hurricane replied when he was asked why he didn't make an effort to block his opponent's punches. "Then I fight better. When I'm hit, man, that's fun!"

And everybody laughed. As long as the commissions allow the likes of Jackson to go on being beaten up for other people's "entertainment," however, it will not be a laughing matter.

When sports columnist Jimmy Cannon defined a club fighter as "one who never takes a backward step on the way to the insane asylum," he pointed out the absurdity of indiscriminate courage. The urge to show the world how tough one is does not always lead to the most edifying results. There was a character named Joe Grimm who fought as a heavyweight in the early years of this century, but he could neither box nor punch. His only "asset" was his astonishing capacity for taking punishment. Feeling that the way to fame and wealth lay along the path of many beatings, Grimm offered his body for sacrifice. He met the leading fighters of his day and boasted, "I am Joe Grimm. I fear no man on earth."

Perhaps the pinnacle of his singular career came one evening in 1903 when he fought Bob Fitzsimmons, one of the greatest of all heavyweight champions. Fitzsimmons had lost his title to Jim Jeffries by this time but he was still one of the deadliest punchers the ring has known. Here the irresistible force met the immovable object. It was a six-round bout and for all of those six rounds Fitzsimmons fired his arsenal of punches at the human punching bag. Blood streaming from countless cuts on his face, his features smashed beyond recognition, his body stamped with ugly bruises, Grimm refused to quit and was still on his feet at the end of the "fight." Staggering to the ropes he held his head as erect as his condition would permit and croaked to the crowd, "I am Joe Grimm. I fear no man on earth."

Like the generals who earn their medals sending thousands of men to their deaths while they remain in protected areas well behind the front lines, the fight managers are natural targets of ironic comment. "They can't hurt us," is the battle-cry typically ascribed to managers as they dispatch their fighters to the slaughter. Heroism by proxy is a traditional part of the prize ring. Managers who have long been associated with game fighters take it as a personal affront when one of their tigers takes the easy way out instead of choosing to be carried home on his shield.

Joe Gould was a prominent manager of the 1920's and '30's, best known for his part in steering Jim Braddock to the heavy-weight championship. On one occasion Gould was asked by another manager, who was going out of town, to handle his heavyweight in an eight-round bout scheduled for a small fight club. Gould agreed to act as the fighter's chief second. The fighter did well enough in the first round but in the second he was hurt by several body punches. Watching him, Gould was certain that the fighter had lost his enthusiasm for the business at hand. He was clearly looking for a way out. He took several more stiff body punches, clinched desperately with his opponent and was a very unhappy-looking young man when he made it back to his corner at the end of the round.

"I hurt my arm," he said to Gould, who was waiting to minister to his bruises in the corner. "I can't go any further."

"You didn't hurt your arm," Gould said, glaring down at him. "Get in there and fight."

"No, honest. I hurt my arm. I can't fight any more."

"Look, you big ——," Gould said through clenched teeth. "You're not going to disgrace me by quitting in *my* corner. If you want to quit, go out there in the middle of the ring and do it."

When the bell rang to start the third round the harried heavyweight got up off his stool, walked to the center of the ring and quit. Gould's record remained without a blot.

We will hear more of Gould later, with a fighter and in circumstances where there was never a chance that he would be disgraced. For our book tells of men like Braddock whose courage was accompanied by the nobility which raised their stories above the usual "who loses and who wins." What is it that sets these men above their rivals? What is the source of those qualities which drove them to overcome the imposing obstacles in their paths? Perhaps Casey Stengel, in speaking of an athlete who shares with the men in our book that unquenchable will to triumph, expressed it most compactly.

Pointing to Enos Slaughter one day, the Yankee manager said:

"He's a good man. He will slide for you and dive for a low hit ball and hit the ground and he will hit the wall for you if he has to. He broke a shoulder for me once trying to make a catch. You can still see the scar right here."

And Stengel sat back and drew an imaginary line across his chest with a firm stroke of his hand. "Slaughter," he said, "was brought up right."

We will turn our attention now to some other men who were brought up right.

Chapter 2 The Yankee Clipper's Return

The uncertainty which haunted the Yankees' training camp in the spring of 1949 was alien to the tradition of this immensely successful ball club. A new manager and a nucleus of aging stars had apparently smothered its purposeful vigor, producing in its followers the melancholy one feels in the presence of decaying splendor. These Yankees, having won the pennant and World Series in 1947, had fallen to third place in 1948. The experts believed they would fall still further in 1949. That Casey Stengel had been named their manager during the off-season seemed to many writers and fans an admission of defeat by Yankee officials, rather than a serious gesture of resistance. Managing wretched National League teams for nine years in Brooklyn and Boston, Casey had never risen out of the second division and had been branded "a perennial loser." It was said that this clown had been hired by the Yankees only to amuse the public while the team was rebuilt. The age and frailty of several key Yankee players would nullify whatever managerial skill he brought to the job.

Easily the most conspicuous of Stengel's frail and aging players was Joe DiMaggio. For years the Yankees had molded their pennant-winning teams around this incomparable center fielder; he was the crutch on which Stengel's predecessors leaned when the team sputtered and stalled. In 1947 he set off the winning drive and in 1948, dragging his reluctant legs through the summer heat, he kept the Yankees in the race with Boston and Cleveland until the final weekend of the season. By then it was apparent that his career was in jeopardy unless the painful bone spur on his right heel was removed. The spur (a calcium deposit) made walking a painful process, and playing ball an almost unbearable one. Joe felt, and the Yankees hoped, that an operation and a winter of rest would put his legs into condition for the 1949 season. The operation to remove the spur, performed in November, 1948, was pronounced a success and DiMag anxiously looked forward to the spring.

When the training camp opened it was natural that Stengel held the spotlight as he took command of his new team. Yet in the background the writers and Yankees players watched DiMag as he tested his heel, for they knew that on his performance would depend the success of the team and, ultimately, Stengel's job. Joe worked out lightly, then returned to the clubhouse and admitted that his heel pained him badly. The hope that traditionally comes with spring quickly waned in the camp of the Yankees.

Team officials, headed by general manager George Weiss, moved swiftly. They ordered DiMaggio to fly to Baltimore's

Johns Hopkins Hospital for a thorough examination of his foot. On March 2, the day after spring training began, Joe was tested by the Baltimore specialists and his heel was pronounced fit to withstand the moderate workouts at St. Petersburg. He was shipped right back to Florida and the news that preceded him there was enough to inject a degree of restrained confidence into the Yankee camp.

Stengel was the only really enthusiastic member of that camp. Having groaned under the burden of mediocrities and worse in Brooklyn and Boston, the gravel-voiced veteran was enchanted by the glitter of the names he now had on his roster. DiMaggio, Tommy Henrich, Phil Rizzuto, Charley Keller—players whose bright skills had lifted the Yankees above their rivals. They were still worthy of respect, though the years seemed to have tarnished their skills. Certainly Stengel accorded them his respect (in DiMaggio's case it sometimes bordered on awe) and he announced to the press that players such as these were free to work themselves into condition as they thought best. For a while it was feared the new manager might have abdicated his authority by his laissez-faire policy; soon the team would be dominating him.

The hope that DiMaggio's troubles were behind him proved an illusion. When the Yankees began to play exhibition games in Florida, Joe tried to stay in the lineup, but invariably the sharp pain in his foot forced him out after several innings. Leaving Florida, the Yankees toured the Gulf states, heading toward Texas. The incision made in Joe's heel the previous November had healed perfectly, but beneath it there was still considerable pain. He could play only two innings at Greenville, Texas, on April 10, then hobbled off the field.

DiMag was desperate. Nothing had worked—rest, whirlpool

baths, heat treatments nor the sponge rubber heels placed in
his shoe. Perhaps Joe himself said it best: "When you come
right down to it, it's not the shoe. It's the —— foot!"

Arriving in Dallas for an exhibition game on April 11, the
Yankees found that the recent rains had left the field damp
and soft. "If I can't play on this field," Joe said to Stengel
before the game, "I can't play on anything. I'll go all out today. I'll give it a real test."

After two and a half innings he gave up. He limped off the
field in agony and the Yankees must have felt then that he
took with him their hopes for the season. The next day he
was on a plane bound for Baltimore, aware that he might
never play ball again. The photographers and reporters realized
it, too, and solemnly recorded the event for posterity. "I looked
so bad I didn't want them to take my picture," Joe said later.
"I looked like a man who had had a nightmare."

This nightmare would torment him for months to come.

It was not a new problem for DiMaggio. His legs and feet
had been a source of trouble to him almost as long as he had
been in professional baseball. As a boy on the sandlots of San
Francisco, where he was born on November 5, 1914, he played
as hard as the other boys and, so far as he can recall, was never
injured. Signed by the San Francisco Seals of the Pacific Coast
League late in 1932, he soon become the brightest prospect on
the West Coast. He was already a marvelous player and it
seemed only a matter of time before one of the big league
teams would buy his contract. One day in 1934, after a game
with Seattle (then managed by an old-time pitcher named
Dutch Ruether), the Seal's trainer walked over to where Joe
sat in the clubhouse and said, "Ruether was talking to me a

little while ago and he wanted to know if you ever hurt your leg."

Joe looked up in surprise. "No," he said, shaking his head. "Why?"

"He says that you drag it when you run."

Joe shook his head again. "I never hurt my leg, and I don't drag it."

"He says you do."

"He's nuts," Joe said, and headed for the shower.

About a week later he was on his way to dinner at his sister's home. The game had been longer than usual, and Joe was late. When the cab drew up in front of the house, he leaped out, and his left knee seemed to explode.

"It popped like a pistol," he was to say years later. "The pain was terrific and I could hardly stand up. I went to a doctor that night and he told me I had pulled a lot of tendons. It bothered me for a long while."

It bothered the big league scouts, too. The boy who had seemed a cinch to become a great player was now a very dubious one, even for a minor league team. He saw little action for the rest of the year and most of the scouts forgot about him. The Seals, who had originally priced their young star's contract at $100,000, were beginning to believe now that they couldn't even give it away. A player with a "trick knee" has a bleak future.

One man had faith in DiMaggio. Bill Essick, the Yankees' West Coast scout, had followed the slender young Italian ever since he had been signed by the Seals. He convinced himself that DiMaggio's knee was strong enough to gamble the money needed to bring Joe to New York. Risking his own reputation, Essick advised the Yankees to buy DiMaggio after the 1934

season. The Seal's only stipulation was that Joe was to remain
in San Francisco during 1935 and report to the Yankees in
the Spring of 1936. And so, for $25,000 and an additional
$15,000 worth of minor league talent, the contract of the
greatest player of his time—and with it the domination of
baseball—passed to the Yankees.

His knee trouble having disappeared over the winter, Joe
returned to the Seals' lineup in the spring of 1935. He got off
to a slow start and brought his batting average up to .320 in
July. Then he became a great ballplayer again. He almost dismantled the league, slugging .500 over the second half of the
season and finishing with a remarkable .398 average. Suddenly
Essick found he had a lot of company on DiMaggio's band-
wagon.

During the winter the word spread eastward from California
that Joe was touched by greatness, and he became one of the
most highly-publicized rookies baseball has had. He had
clinched a job in the Yankee outfield even before he reported
for the first time to the Yankees' training camp at St. Petersburg. The eyes of old-timers at that camp glowed in his
presence like those of butterfly collectors at the sight of the
rarest of specimens. He was not a showoff, nor even a spectacular player in the sense that Ty Cobb and Jackie Robinson
were spectacular. The sense of excitement which possessed
those who watched him came from the easy grace with which
he played; he had the controlled rhythm of a ballet dancer and
the deceptive agility of a young animal.

He also had the confidence which is a part of every magnificent performer. When asked by the writers at the start of
the official season how he expected to adjust to the stiffer
competition in the American League, Joe, in the modest tones

that were his by nature, replied that he thought he would be helped by, among other things, the better umpiring. "The umpires up here don't call many wrong," he said. "You don't have to swing at balls that just miss the plate because you're afraid they'll be called strikes. You can let them alone. That way you get more good ones to hit."

Babe Ruth had been gone from Yankee Stadium only a year and it was a tribute to the twenty-one-year-old DiMaggio that the Yankees looked to him to lead them back to the top of the baseball world. His early performance in camp left little doubt that he would do just that. He was an amazing player, combining his sharp batting eye with terrific power at the plate. He was a smart and swift runner on the bases and his strong throwing arm and uncanny defensive ability made him the greatest center fielder since Tris Speaker. Then, just as it seemed that he would help the Yankees to their fastest start in years, the imp that so often marred his springtimes popped out of nowhere.

Joe had suffered a minor foot injury in an exhibition game. The Yankee trainer, feeling that heat treatment would speed his recovery, placed DiMag's left foot in a diathermy machine. Evidently Joe's skin was extremely sensitive and, when the foot was taken out, it was broiled like a steak. Two huge and ugly blisters kept Joe idle for many weeks and he was out of the lineup when the Yankees opened the regular season.

When he did return he was an immediate sensation. Joining Lou Gehrig and Bill Dickey in the lineup, he contributed his share toward making it the new "Murderers' Row." The Yankees were off and running toward the first of four consecutive pennants and World Series they would win under manager Joe McCarthy from 1936 through 1939. In recogni-

tion of the manner in which these sluggers took turns obliterat-
ing the opposition, one press-box versifier made an abortive
reach for immortality with the following lines:

> Ashes to ashes and dust to dust;
> If Gehrig and Dickey don't, DiMaggio must.

And, just as important to a professional baseball team, Joe
became an irresistible attraction at the box office. For the first
time the large Italian populations in the cities that made up the
American League took an interest in baseball. They flocked
to Yankee Stadium and other ball parks, carrying big banners
and Italian flags which they unfolded and waved whenever
their hero performed the spectacular—as he so often did. At
the ticket windows they asked for a seat "near where DiMag
plays." Another poet, closer to the people, perhaps, scribbled
this very mortal couplet:

> DiMaggio's triple
> Aroused da pipple.

Joe was selected for the American League all-star team in
his rookie year; in 1937 he hit 46 home runs to lead the
league; and he won the batting championship in 1939 with an
average of .381. He had fulfilled his immeasurable promise and
was now the greatest player in the game. The Yankees faltered
briefly in 1940 (though Joe again won the batting title) and
they obviously needed a lift in 1941. DiMaggio was equal
to the job and set a fire under the team with one of the most
remarkable achievements in big league history.

On May 15 Joe made one hit in four times at bat against
Chicago at the Stadium. It was only a single and seemed in-
significant at the time. But, as day after day passed and Di-
Maggio kept getting his base hits, the statistic hunters realized

he had a chance to tie or smash the forty-four-year-old record for hits in consecutive games, established by Willie Keeler of the old Baltimore Orioles. Willie had hit in 44 straight games. As Joe approached the mark, perhaps the most extraordinary record in the books because of the almost unbearable pressure under which the player must perform every day, the crowds flocked to see him and prayed and rooted for him to get his hit.

The critical day was July 1. Playing against the Red Sox, Joe slashed two hits in the first game of a doubleheader to tie the record, then came back in the second game with a single to break it. Even the experienced and allegedly cynical writers rose from their seats in the press box and beat the palms of their hands raw in a rare tribute to an outstanding player. It was only after 56 games that the long batting streak was finally snuffed out.

DiMaggio was a strange titan. Painfully shy, he had none of the bluff good humor or colorful habits and gestures of that earlier titan, Babe Ruth. Joe seemed at ease only on the ball field. Sitting in a New York restaurant one evening, he listened silently to his teammate, Vernon "Goofy" Gomez, tell funny stories and swap good-natured wisecracks with the newspapermen. Later Joe said to a friend, "I'd give anything if I could do that."

He did not mix often with the other Yankee players and some of them resented his aloofness. This aloofness, however, was not a pose. It was always hard for him to make friends and away from the ball park he spent most of his time with a couple of the old pals he had met in New York early in his career. The idol of millions, he was an intensely lonely man. "Everyone has a home and a family to go to," he once said to a writer after a game at the Stadium. "All I've got when I go back to my hotel tonight is an empty room and a box of fresh laundry on the bed."

And yet this man, who lived within the walls his shyness had raised, was forced to move always in the glare of publicity off the field and to be the inspirational leader of his team on it. As one of his friends pointed out, Joe lived for years in New York and never rode on the subway; so distinctive was his face that he would have been immediately recognized and mobbed. Living in a hotel, he ate most of his meals in restaurants, and time after time his food grew cold as he signed menus, business cards and scraps of paper for the unthinking thousands who wanted his autograph. When he stepped onto the street for a stroll in the fresh air, every head turned to stare at him and he was followed for blocks by shouting children. He could not sip a ginger ale in a night club without inciting rumors that he was a lush.

The familiar saying in New York that "As DiMag goes, so go the Yankees" was as true as it was trite. He had the capacity to lift a slumping ball club and carry it along on his own wonderful play; and his teammates invariably responded to his effort by performing as they never did without him. Connie Mack once said of him: "As one of nine men, DiMaggio is the best player that ever lived." What Mack meant was that there have been greater individual players, perhaps, but never one who contributed so much to the success of his team. His skill in every phase of the game, his incomparable baseball instinct and his ability to serve as the inspirational leader of his teammates set him apart from every other man who has played baseball.

Joe Page, the fine relief pitcher who roomed with DiMag

for several years, once indicated the reverence in which "The Yankee Clipper" was held by his teammates. "As long as I can remember," Page said, "when the Yankees took the field, they all waited for Joe to make the first break. Nothing was said about this ritual, but everybody held back and waited for Joe to lead us out."

Like most great athletes, DiMag often went out of his way to give a lift to the opposition, too. When the Yankees played the Philadelphia Phillies in the 1950 World Series, they hopped off to a quick lead by winning the first two games. The Phils, made up chiefly of younger players who had been called "The Whiz Kids" by the reporters, were trying hard to get back into the Series by taking the third game. They led, 2-1, in the eighth inning. Then the Yankees rallied and got the tying run to third base. DiMag was on first. The next batter hit an easy grounder at Granny Hamner. In his anxiety to make the important out, the young shortstop fumbled the ball and allowed the tying run to score. Hamner stood stunned near second base, vaguely hearing the hoots of the crowd. DiMag, turning, saw the look on the boy's face.

"Don't worry about it, Granny," he said gently. "It happens to the best of them."

And so there was good cause for the gloom which hung over the Yankees as they opened the 1949 season. The Yankees without DiMaggio were scarcely Yankees at all. It was true that this was the sixth opening game which he had missed in his eleven seasons at the Stadium (he was in the Army for three years during World War II), but these injuries were coming regularly now. Before the 1947 season there had been an operation on his left heel and before the 1948 season there had been an operation to remove the bone chips from his right elbow; neither operation had troubled him like this one. "You don't suppose I'm falling apart, do you?" he glumly asked a friend in the hospital.

The writers and most of Joe's teammates believed he was. A similar heel ailment had ended the career of Rogers Hornsby, a player considered by many people to have been rivaled only by DiMaggio among the right-handed hitters baseball has known. It seemed unlikely that, at thirty-four, Joe could make a comeback, especially as he had missed almost all of the invaluable conditioning period in the spring and was certain to miss so much of the regular season. And, without DiMag, it was felt that the question of Stengel's ability as a manager would go unresolved.

Yet the same attitude which had brought Joe to grief in the first place—the competitive drive which refused to allow him to favor his legs and give anything but his best when the heel trouble developed—gave him at least a chance now against overwhelming odds. He was fiercely determined to play ball again.

First there were days in the hospital as the doctors worked on the heel, and then long days and nights in his New York hotel room, sitting impatiently in front of a television set or brooding quietly alone. He avoided everyone but his few close friends. His heel still pained him and that made him grumpy and whenever he stepped out of his room there was some well-meaning idiot ready with a special remedy for all of his ailments. And then in May there was a moment of tragedy; his father died in San Francisco. It was the bleakest period of DiMaggio's life.

The Yankees were away to a surprisingly fast start.

Stengel, using every trick he had picked up in forty years of baseball, juggled his aging players with a dubious collection of castoffs and rookies and the Yankees moved off in first place. The powerful Boston Red Sox, heavily favored to win the pennant, floundered badly and, with the head start the Yankees had, Stengel became convinced his chances of victory were good. If only he had a sound Joe DiMaggio! His team, as it shaped up now, did not appear capable of holding on much past mid-season.

One morning in May DiMaggio let himself out of bed, expecting to feel the usual sharp pain in his heel, and was thrilled to discover that there was not a trace of soreness. He moved gingerly about his room that day, and his heel remained miraculously free from pain.

He was given permission to work out lightly at the Stadium. He climbed into his pin-striped Yankee uniform with the big black number 5 on the back and, wearing a specially constructed right shoe that carried spikes only on the toe, trotted out on the field several hours before the Yankees were to play a night game on May 23. There were a few fans already in the stands. When they recognized the great center fielder, they sent up a delighted cheer which rolled through the empty spaces of the big stadium. Joe took batting practice for a few minutes, raising blisters on the hands that by now were so unaccustomed to the feel of wood. Then he jogged easily in the outfield, caught a couple of fly balls and finally went back into the clubhouse. The crowd, larger now, applauded him once more. His heel had successfully passed its first test.

"This suit feels so good I think I'll wear it to bed," he told the reporters in the clubhouse. "I'm in uniform to stay."

Despite his determination and optimism, he knew it would

be several weeks before he could try to play. He had lost
weight during the spring and his legs, having missed the hard
work every player needs in Florida, were weak. The most the
Yankees could hope for was that Joe would be ready for an
occasional game by the middle of July.

Joe worked and fretted and the Yankees held grimly to their
lead. Behind them, however were the Red Sox, alive now and
slamming the ball as the experts had said they would back in
the early spring. Stengel had originally planned to ease DiMag
into the lineup, using him occasionally as a pinch hitter. Now,
encouraged by the unexpected speed with which Joe was re-
gaining his strength, Casey had a change of heart. "I won't
use him until he's ready to play every day," he told the writers.
"I want all of Joe, or nothing."

The Yankees played the New York Giants in a charity exhibition game at the Stadium on Monday night, June 27. Di-
Maggio went to Stengel before the game and told him he
wanted to play.

Casey's homely face, always expressive, took on a glow that
was unusual even for him. "All right, but take it easy tonight,"
he said. "Try it for a couple of innings, and then I'll put somebody else in."

Joe started and, as the innings passed, his legs did not weaken.
When Stengel looked at him after the fifth inning, Joe indicated with a nod that he wanted to remain in the game. He
played the full distance and was tired but happy afterwards
in the clubhouse, although he had gone hitless in four times
at bat against a knuckleball pitcher named Kirby Higbe. A
knuckler is difficult to hit under any conditions and Joe was
sure that his hitting would improve as he regained his timing.
His heel felt fine. That was the main thing.

The Yankees were to leave the next day for an important three-game series in Boston. The Red Sox had won nine of their last ten games. They were rolling now, and it seemed inevitable that they would overhaul the Yankees before July 4. DiMag told Stengel that if his heel did not swell up overnight he would be ready to open the series in Boston. He felt all right the next morning but he wasn't on the train when the Yankees left. Perhaps, now that the moment for a decision had come, he was reluctant to make it. A player who has missed the first sixty-five games of a season and then is expected to lead his team in a critical series must be aware of the imposing burden he carries. Joe left his hotel, had lunch at Toots Shor's restaurant and convinced himself that he was ready. He took a three-fifteen plane for Boston and arrived in the clubhouse at Fenway Park just after five o'clock.

Certainly the Yankees, sorely pressed by their chief opposition, got a tremendous psychological lift from DiMaggio's presence. Even the early arrivals among the noisily pro-Boston crowd greeted Joe's appearance on the field with a cheer.

"Go get 'em, Joe!"

"Atta boy, Joe!"

He walked into the batting cage and rifled practice pitches against and over the left field wall. Stengel, who did not yet know for certain that Joe would play, watched the long drives in awe. "I hope he plays," he growled to a writer standing next to him. "I like to watch him hit."

Joe walloped one more ball over the wall, and then left the cage. As he walked back to the dugout he nodded to Stengel and the Yankee manager made out his lineup. The name of Joe DiMaggio was in it for the first time that season.

There were 36,228 fans in the stands as the game began.

Allie Reynolds was the Yankee pitcher, facing the hard-throwing Mickey McDermott of the Red Sox. DiMaggio received a loud cheer as he came to bat in the second inning and, in storybook fashion, lined a single to left. Johnny Lindell walked and, when Hank Bauer crashed a home run, the Yankees led, 3-0. In the third inning Phil Rizzuto walked and was on base when DiMag made his second appearance at the plate. He was greeted by an even louder cheer. A moment later the crowd was in an uproar. The Yankee Clipper, waiting for the pitch he wanted, his feet spread in that famous stance, tore into one of McDermott's fast balls. The ball sailed high over Ted Williams' head in left field and landed in the screen above the wall for his first home run of the season.

Perhaps not even that long wallop was as much of an indication of DiMaggio's greatness as a minor incident which took place in the eighth inning. Joe, who had grounded out in his third time at bat, came up for the last time in the eighth and walked. Yogi Berra then hit a sharp grounder to second baseman Bobby Doerr for what looked like the start of a routine double play. Doerr scooped the ball to shortstop Vern Stephens for the force on DiMag, and Stephens set himself for the throw to first base. He never got it off. Completely disregarding his fragile leg, the Yankee centerfielder hurled himself at Stephens in a rolling block, upsetting him and ruining his chance to complete the double play.

Meanwhile the Red Sox nibbled away at the Yankee lead. The score was 5-3 as the two teams battled into the ninth inning, and the Sox drove out Reynolds before he could retire a batter. DiMaggio's roommate, Joe Page, came in at this point, with two men on and nobody out. One of the runners scored on a fly ball and then, with two out and the tying run on base,

Ted Williams came to bat. It was a dramatic finish for an intensely dramatic game. Williams hit the ball hard, but it was to deep center field and DiMaggio, running easily with those long strides, went back and pulled it down.

"I'm glad they didn't tie it up then," Joe said in the clubhouse a few minutes later. "I was so tired, I couldn't go another inning."

The Yankees had temporarily halted their rivals, but there were still two games to play in the series. Their confidence bolstered by their star's amazing performance in that first game, the Yanks hoped to crush Boston by sweeping the series.

The Red Sox were still dangerous. They pounced on the New York pitchers early in the second game and built up a commanding 7-1 lead. In the fifth inning the Yankees got two runners on base and DiMaggio, hitless up to this point, came to bat. He pounded the ball over the left field wall for a home run and the Yankees were back in the game. Elated now, his teammates came swinging back and tied the score, 7-7. That was how it stood when Joe came to bat again in the eighth.

There were two out and nobody was on base as he faced a lefthander named Earl Johnson. The Boston pitcher got his curve ball over the plate and DiMag sent it soaring high over the screen and into the street beyond the left field wall. This was the winning run. The Yankees added one more and won, 9-7.

Now it seemed that the whole country had turned to look at Boston. People who couldn't tell you where first base was knew that an amazing athlete named Joe DiMaggio had returned, as it were, from the dead, and was performing the kind of feats which have stirred men's hearts for as long as they have cared about courage in the face of disheartening odds.

A country's affection, denied him because of his aloofness in the days of his youth and strength, had come to him as time ran out.

There was one more game. Vic Raschi, a determined competitor, pitched for the Yankees and led, 3-2, at the end of six innings. The Red Sox had kept him in trouble, however, and it was unlikely that he could protect his slim margin. The Yankees could expect little help from Page, their relief ace, either, as he had pitched hard in the first two games of the series. Yankee second baseman George Stirnweiss opened the eighth with a single, and moved to second on a hit by Tommy Henrich. The next hitter was DiMaggio. The tension in the old ball park grew almost unbearable as the Boston pitcher, Mel Parnell, worked carefully on Joe. The count went to three-and-two. Parnell had to come in with his next pitch and DiMaggio drove it high into the light tower above the left field wall for his mightiest home run of the series. It proved to be the winning blow. The Red Sox scored once more, but the Yankees won, 6-3.

This was more than a heartwarming and dramatic performance by a player whose greatness had seemed to be leaving him. It was eventually to bring a pennant and a world championship to Yankee Stadium. Stengel, who had been called a clown and a second-division manager, brought his team of shreds and patches home in first place, one game ahead of the Red Sox, on October 2. It was, one writer said, "Casey's greatest gag." And that three-game sweep in Boston, which knocked back what might have been the Red Sox's winning drive, was certainly DiMaggio's most glorious achievement.

Joe will live in the memories of baseball fans for many, many reasons—the easy grace with which he pursued long fly balls, his uncanny skill at taking the extra base on an unwary enemy outfielder, his remarkable fifty-six-game hitting streak and (a good reason, too) his brief marriage to Marilyn Monroe. But no other memory will erase that of the crippled star, coming out of the dugout when he was most desperately needed, to turn back the surging Red Sox. That is what every sport is all about.

Chapter 3 **The Game**

Flurries of wet snow blew out of the cold, damp sky, melting quickly into the muddy field and chilling the 58,000 people in Harvard Stadium. It was November 20, 1937, and the crowd was there to watch football's most important traditional spectacle, the Yale-Harvard game. The ancient glory of the rivalry, with its long list of heroes and memorable events over the years, gives it a unique drama. But this year the game was something special. It pitted a Harvard team that, as the season moved into its closing weeks, had proved itself one of the best in the school's history against a Yale squad whose incomparable half-back, Clint Frank, had guided it unbeaten through its first eight games.

Frank was aware of the odds his team must overcome to beat Harvard. The most modest of athletes, he nevertheless knew that Yale depended completely on him for its success, and the long difficult season already had taken much out of him. Yale's line was no match for Harvard's, a beautifully drilled, hard-charging unit that would hound Frank from the opening gun. Clint had already listened to one scout's pre-game report on Harvard: "I've seen all the top teams in the East this fall," the man had said, "but Harvard is the only team I've *heard* play football." When the Crimson line hit a ball carrier, the sound carried to the topmost rows of the stadium.

As he sat in the clubhouse, the yards of tape and bandages on his body testifying to the beating he had taken during the season, Frank's awareness of the obstacle ahead of him was overridden by his immense pride in the accomplishments of this Yale team. He was its captain, an honor which he took very seriously. And this team, whose lack of depth in the line was a severe handicap, had compiled a record marred only by a tie with Dartmouth; even then Yale's last-second rally against a powerful foe had permitted Frank and his teammates to walk off the field with a moral victory. Now, playing his last game for Yale and leading his team against their ancient rivals, Frank wanted victory more than ever before. The eyes of every person in the stands would be on him throughout the game. What was more important, and more ominous, the eyes of that formidable Harvard line would be on him too.

The Yale fans in the crowd set up a loud cheer as they saw Frank, the white number 14 standing out on his blue jersey, trotting onto the field. There was not an empty seat in the ivy-draped stadium. Speculators near the gates were offering tickets for sale at fifty dollars apiece, a tremendous sum in those post-Depression years, and they were finding eager buyers.

Harvard, making certain to keep the ball away from Frank,

kicked off to Yale's quarterback, Charlie Ewart, and the game was on. Each team played cautiously on the wet field, exchanging punts and trying to force the break that might lead to a sudden score. Harvard's one bold stroke in the opening period was frustrated by Frank. The Crimson's best passer, Frank Foley, spotted a receiver in the open at mid-field and fired the ball in his direction. Frank, moving rapidly on the sodden field, rushed in to bat down the pass.

A moment later Harvard punted and Frank ran the ball all the way back to his opponents' 34-yard line. Yale was suddenly in position to score. But here Harvard's magnificent line rose to meet the threat and Yale finally relinquished the ball. From that moment on Harvard dominated the first half. Yet, despite the superiority of the Harvard team, Frank was unquestionably the standout player on the field.

The crowd, huddled in slickers against the wind and snow, thrilled to the great back's performance. When Harvard punted and the wet ball bounced crazily toward the Yale goal line, Frank boldly rushed into the circle of Crimson players hovering over it, snatched it up and ran it back to midfield. One of Yale's few important gains during the half came when Frank made a marvelous catch of a pass by Ewart, lunging to pluck the ball almost off the grass near the sidelines. Twice the Harvard line opened huge holes through which its hard-running backs broke into the open; both times Frank, the only player that stood between the runner and a touchdown, brought the crowd to its feet with diving tackles.

But even Frank's brilliance was not enough to keep Harvard from crossing the Yale goal. A long pass from Foley to end Don Daughters put Harvard ahead, 6-0, and that was the score as the two teams, their uniforms wet and muddy, trudged

off the field for their half-time rest. The Yale rooters who rose
to applaud their team realized that the game would now be a
rout had it not been for the play of Frank. Running, passing,
tackling, blocking, pass defending and calling the signals, he
was a heroic and inspiring figure. "It's risky picking any team
against Clint Frank," Stanley Woodward had written while
predicting a Harvard victory in the New York *Herald Tribune*
before the game, and now 58,000 people had seen how much
this one great player meant to his team.

This final half at Harvard Stadium was to mark the climax
of Frank's football career. Those who knew him best realized
it was a remarkable achievement that he had ever played a
single game for Yale. But it was the same unquenchable determination to succeed that still made him a dangerous obstacle to
Harvard when all of the other trump cards were in their
hands. Though he was weary and limping, there would be no
relief for Frank. Al Wilson, Yale's right halfback, was in bed
with pneumonia and the team's only other dependable halfback, Al Hessberg, who could have spelled Frank occasionally,
would have to fill Wilson's spot.

"Call Hessberg's number more often," Yale coach Ducky
Pond, walking over to Frank, said. "You can't go much
farther on that leg and maybe we can shake Hessberg loose
while they're trying to bottle you up."

Yet Pond knew that, if Yale was to win, it would be Frank
who would make the difference. Frank was greatest under
the most intense pressure, coolest at the most critical moment.
He had already come back from disheartening injuries to be
recognized as the finest back in Yale history. National recognition was his, too, and he would win the Heisman Trophy
that fall as the country's outstanding college player.

For a time it had seemed unlikely that he would be able to go out for football at Yale. His schoolboy exploits in Evanston, Illinois, promised an exciting career for him, but a shoulder injury had dimmed his hopes. He did not play football at Lawrenceville, where he prepped for Yale, nor even on the Yale freshman team. Yet, coming out for the varsity as a sophomore, this rugged young man became a sensation. He made several spectacular touchdown runs in the early games but, once again, he was hampered by an injury, this time to his ankle, and he was of little help for the remainder of the year.

The experts had seen enough, however. They knew that a sound Clint Frank could rise to greatness. He did not look the part of an All-America halfback—at first glance, that is. Wearing glasses and dressing conservatively, he resembled a divinity student or, perhaps, an economics major, which he happened to be. But, at five feet ten inches and 190 pounds, he was constructed like a baby tank. He hit with a terrific power on the football field, and yet had amazing speed and elusiveness.

In 1936, his junior year, Frank teamed with Larry Kelley in one of the most famous of all forward passing combinations. Kelley was a standout player, an end who had a remarkable ability to catch passes and an even more remarkable knack for being in the right place at the right time. Glib, spectacular and, with it all, immensely talented, Kelley naturally grabbed the headlines. Frank's tremendous all-around ability was often overlooked while Kelley kept the spotlight on himself. Larry even forced the rulemakers to rewrite the books. Against Navy, spotting a loose ball in the midst of a group of enemy players, he rushed in, booted it away from them in the manner of a soccer player trying for a goal, and set up a Yale touch-

down when the fumbled ball was finally recovered deep in
Navy territory.

It was a tribute to Frank's skills that he gained equal recognition with the flamboyant Kelley late in the season. These
two Yale immortals brought their team a Big Three championship with thrilling performances against Princeton and Harvard. Yale fell behind a strong Princeton team in the first half
and trailed by an apparently hopeless score of 16-0. Then, just
before the end of the half, Frank crashed over for a touchdown. Hessberg scored in the third quarter to cut the margin
still further and then the marvelous Frank-to-Kelley passing
attack went into action. They dazzled the Princeton secondary
with their specialty, and finally Kelley got into the clear and
took a pass from Clint which put the Bulldogs ahead, 20-16.

Princeton, still very much alive, fought back in the fourth
period and recaptured the lead, 23-20. Now the game went into
its closing minutes. Frank, eating up the yards by crashing
through the Tiger line or tossing his soft, accurate passes to
the nimble Kelley, brought the ball into scoring position. With
the crowd in an uproar, he finally carried it across the goal for
the touchdown which brought Yale an amazing 26-23 victory.

The same combination brought Yale a 14-13 victory over
Harvard the following week. A long run by Frank set up
Yale's first score in the second period. A few moments later
he passed to Kelley in the end zone for what appeared to be
another touchdown. But a penalty against the Yale line nulli-
fied the score. When the ball had been set back to Harvard's
42, Frank calmly stepped back and tossed another pass to
Kelley and this time the touchdown counted.

As the 1937 season opened, the Yale team was a mystery.
There would be no Larry Kelley to pop up at the critical

moment with an unexpected play. The entire burden would be on Frank, and there were many who felt his effectiveness would be sharply restricted when there was no Kelley there to catch his passes and no solid front line to open up the holes for his bull-like rushes. Whatever success Yale would have would be up to him. The odds were heavily against him.

The season quickly became a series of personal triumphs for this remarkable player. He was not a one-man team, of course. The line, though not outstanding, played with spirit and gave him valuable blocking. Fullback Dave Colwell was an excellent kicker and blocker, and the other backs, Charlie Ewart, Wilson and Hessberg, were good runners. But it was to Frank that Yale had to look in its moments of crisis. No man ever contributed more to his team.

Yale opened the season by beating a stubborn University of Maine team, 26-0, and Frank was responsible for three of the four touchdowns, scoring the first himself and passing for two others. Pennsylvania, with its experienced line, provided a greater challenge, but Frank was equal to it. Immediately after the opening kickoff, Clint completed a forward pass to put the ball in Penn territory, then gained 36 yards on two rushing plays to bring the ball to Penn's 12-yard line. A moment later he passed for the first touchdown. Later he intercepted a Penn pass and raced it back 61 yards for another touchdown. The Bulldogs won the game 27-7, and Frank's all-around play was the chief topic of conversation afterward. As Leo Riordan wrote in the Philadelphia *Ledger:*

"Frank, the 'Rhapsody in Blue,' is no doubt the greatest player of the year. He is the All-America backfield by himself. It would have been a good game if he had gone fishing. Penn weakened herself by continually throwing passes into Frank's territory, because he was the best pass-interceptor in the game today."

Yale continued to baffle the experts, decisively beating a strong Army team the following week, 15-7, as Frank passed to one touchdown and twice cut off Army scores by making jarring tackles in the open field. Playing Cornell on a muddy field the next week, Frank scored the only touchdown on an amazing 68-yard run and Yale won, 9-0.

The Dartmouth game provided one of the highlights of the season. Yale trailed, 9-2, with only a minute to play. Frank, cool under pressure, completed a pass to Hessberg for a first down on Dartmouth's 35. Now there was only a half minute to play. Frank threw three long passes, each of which was batted down by alert Dartmouth defenders. Now it was fourth down and there were but twelve seconds to go. Frank, calling the plays, took the ball himself and, dodging the fast-charging Dartmouth linemen, picked out Hessberg in the open field and threw a perfect pass into his arms. Hessberg gathered it in and raced into the end zone for a touchdown. When Gil Humphrey kicked the extra point, Frank and his teammates walked off the field with a 9-9 tie.

Concentrating on his running in Yale's next game, Frank took Brown apart. He gained almost 200 yards rushing and scored all three of Yale's touchdowns in a 19-0 victory. Clint was even better the next week against Princeton. In a fierce storm that made it improbable that a man could maneuver on the soggy field, he raced to four touchdowns, two of them on runs of 79 and 52 yards. The final score was 26-0. In the New York *Herald Tribune* the next day, Jesse Abramson wrote: "In this storm, the worst the Bowl has known in five years, Frank delivered a heroic performance that defies belief. Unruffled by the worst the elements could offer, the electrifying leader of this grand Yale team drove his mates to a stunning triumph."

And Ewart, Frank's teammate, said of him: "What a terrific second effort Frank has. They think they have him stopped, then Clint gives it that extra push and all of a sudden he's away again."

"It's funny the things that come into your mind when you look back on a certain period of your life," Frank said recently. "When I think back to my days at Yale it's not the touchdowns I scored or the passes I threw that I think about. The most vivid memory of football I have comes from that rainy day when we played Princeton. I had just scored my fourth touchdown and we went back into a huddle before trying for the extra point. Frank Gallagher, a wonderful kid who was the center on our team and who later was killed in the war, looked up and said:

" 'I say that instead of place-kicking we should try to punt the ball clear out of the Bowl.'

"Maybe it sounds silly now, but with that rain pouring down and the rest of us feeling good because we were so far ahead, we all burst out laughing. And that's what I remember most about playing football at Yale."

And now Frank had reached his last game. Though failure in this one could not mar the reputation he had built for himself, a victory would mean a great deal to him. As Yale's captain, he would be proud to lead his team to triumph against Harvard in what had come to be known as THE GAME. Listening to Coach Pond's last few words of instruction, Frank checked the special guards which protected his injured right

shoulder and knee, then strapped on his big white helmet and
went out on the field.

Harvard kicked off to start the second half. The ball bounced
near the Yale goal and Frank, coming up quickly, grabbed it
and bulled his way up the field to Yale's 35. Two long runs
by Hessberg brought the ball deep into Harvard territory and
Frank, driving hard, scored on a buck from the two-yard line.
The score was 6-6 and the Yale supporters in the crowd had
gained new hope.

A few moments later Yale's chances for victory all but
flickered out. Frank's knee was badly wrenched, making it
almost impossible for him to run with any speed or deception.
"The knee was so badly swollen," umpire Tom Thorpe said
later, "that he was barely able to move. I couldn't see how
the fellow could make another play. He could start only on
one leg. The injury was enough to make two iron men call it
a day."

But Frank refused to give up. He remained the bulwark of
Yale's defense. Harvard's line was opening up big holes again
and those fleet backs were coming through on spinners, eating
up the yards toward the Yale goal. But time after time Frank
rushed up from the secondary to plug the hole and bring down
the ball carrier. When Harvard passed, Frank somehow re-
versed his field and faded back to break up the plays.

Near the end of the third period Yale got a break. A Harvard
back fumbled one of Colwell's punts and it was recovered on
the Crimson's 24. Now the Harvard line stiffened and appeared
about to take back the ball on downs. But, on fourth down,
Frank called his own signal, drove forward and, with a mighty
effort, made a first down on Harvard's 12. The gun went off
ending the third period and the two teams changed goals to

begin the final quarter. Here an offside penalty hurt Yale and, with the attack stymied after three downs, Frank called for a field goal. Colwell's try from the 20 failed, and Harvard took possession of the ball.

It was Yale's last real chance. The line had been worn down by Harvard's ceaseless battering and could put up little resistance. The Crimson backs broke through for big gains and, as often as not, their way was barred only by the ever-present Frank. Then, with the ball on Yale's ten-yard line, Harvard's Foley started off tackle. Frank came up to plug the hole and Foley, cutting sharply, swept around end and headed for the goal line. With Frank effectively out of the play now, Foley had a clear field ahead of him and he went over standing up. The extra point was kicked and Harvard led, 13-6.

This was almost certainly the winning score; if there were to be any more touchdowns, it was likely that Harvard would score them, too. But Frank rallied his team and fought back. Bud Humphrey was sent into the game to do the passing for the Bulldogs, allowing their two best runners, Frank and Hessberg, to go downfield as receivers. Frank limped badly whenever he moved, but the Harvard defenders still feared him. They covered him closely each time he went out.

The snow had turned to rain now and, in the gathering darkness of a late New England afternoon, the ball was more slippery and more difficult to see than before. Once Frank leaped high between two Harvard defenders to pluck the wet ball out of the air with one hand, then went crashing to the ground as his knee buckled under him. In the waning minutes of the game Yale, still battling, reached Harvard's 25. Then four desperation passes by Humphrey failed and Harvard took over the ball. As the last seconds were ticked off, Harvard students poured onto the field and began to tear down the goal posts.

The game was over. As the gun sounded, Frank, who had played the entire sixty minutes, collapsed. Two of his teammates rushed to his side and, helping him to stay on his feet, led him toward the sidelines. Other Yale players gathered around him to keep away the mobs of idolizing fans who were trying to get to him to slap him on the back and tell him how marvelous he had been. Others, standing on their seats in the rain and wind, looked down on the jubilant torchlit parade of Harvard students tramping rapidly across the field, and, on the other side, the slow-moving group of players in muddy blue jerseys who surrounded the weary, beaten Yale halfback.

Clint Frank, in victory, had been one of Yale's all-time stars; in defeat, he had added one of the most stirring chapters to the history of American football.

Chapter 4 **Last Chance**

There is one baseball gag that has never become dated. Uni-form styles change, players come and go, franchises are dis-lodged and the ball itself varies in resiliency. But you can be sure that every once in a while some press-box wit will reach down and pull out this hoary chestnut: "Washington—first in war, first in peace, and last in the American League."

As the Yankees are associated with baseball success, so Washington is almost synonymous with abject failure. Brook-lyn fans won a nation's sympathy bewailing the inadequacies of their "Bums," but not even the most loyal citizen of Flat-bush would have had the boundless capacity for suffering needed to watch the Senators over a period of years. Wash-ington fans are truly the martyrs of baseball. Occasionally the team rises from the depths of the American League to snatch a breath of higher, purer air. But these are temporary surges, plateaus of success in a wasteland of defeat. In the early years of this century, as in our own time, the Senators were chiefly noted for their ingenuity in devising ways to lose ball games.

This is the story of Walter Johnson of the Washington Senators. "The Big Train," they called him, and he captured the imagination of the public as no other pitcher has before or since. He was the Babe Ruth of the mound. As the mention of the Babe's name summoned in one's mind the vision of towering home runs, so the name Walter Johnson meant, for several generations of fans, an overpowering fast ball. A Detroit batter (legend holds that it was Ping Bodie), having taken his three futile swings at the spot he judged Johnson's pitches to be, walked slowly back to the dugout and tossed his bat aside in resignation. "You can't hit what you can't see," he said, and those words should have been carved into Johnson's tombstone after his death in 1946. They summed up the despair of thousands of batters who faced Johnson when he was the most impressive pitcher in baseball.

And yet it was Johnson's misfortune to spend most of his big league career with a miserable ball club. For five years after he joined the Senators in 1907, the team could not rise above seventh place; for many of the rest of the twenty-one seasons he pitched in Washington the team was battling, often unsuccessfully, to stay out of the second division. When he soared to his most brilliant triumphs, he pulled what was the dead weight of his team up behind him. And too often his incompetent teammates pulled him down after them. He pitched in the astonishing total of sixty 1-0 games, and he won forty of them. No wonder that his thousands of fans despaired of ever seeing him fulfill his fondest wish—to pitch and win a World Series game. "First in war, first in peace, and last in

the American League." Maybe it *was* funny, but not to Walter
Johnson.

Perhaps the most stirring spectacle a sport can offer, and
certainly its most valuable lesson, is that of a great performer
toiling heroically in a hopeless cause. Those who watched
Johnson in his prime have never been able to forget him:
usually scorning any other pitch but his incomparable fast
ball, overlooking the mistakes of his teammates, accepting
every decision of the umpires without a word of rebuke or
self-pity, and all the while winning more games (413) than
any other pitcher in the history of the American League and
striking out more batters (3,497) than any other pitcher who
ever lived. He was an appealing man and a devastating pitcher.

The fast ball, launched by his famous side-arm delivery, was
what they will remember him for. Ty Cobb was talking about
Johnson once, and he said, "You knew you were going to get
that fast ball every time you faced him. You never had to guess.
You could get set for it, but you still couldn't hit him. Walter
was the fastest."

That was the comment of a man who is called by many the
greatest hitter the game has known. An even more impartial
observer was Billy Evans, an outstanding umpire for many
years in the American League. Speaking of Johnson, Billy
made what was, for an umpire, a unique admission. "He was
the only pitcher who made me close my eyes instinctively as
his pitch came at me. When I was umpiring behind the plate I
tried to glue my eyes to every pitch, but his were too much for
me. I remember once when Joe Gideon of the Yankees was at
bat. The last time I saw it this pitch of Johnson's looked like
it was going to be a strike. So that's the way I called it. Gideon
looked back at me, kind of blinking, and he said, 'What was it,
a fast ball or a curve?'

" 'Why ask me about it?' I said.

"He shrugged and grinned. 'I never saw it. I had to close my eyes.'

"That made me feel better. I knew the ballplayers couldn't second guess me if they were closing their eyes, too."

Johnson's fast ball was the yardstick against which all other pitches were measured. When a talented youngster came to the big leagues no finer compliment could be paid him than to say that he was "almost as fast as Johnson." Lefty Grove, Dizzy Dean and Bob Feller were all compared in their prime to "The Big Train." They were "almost as fast." In his short story "Horseshoes" Ring Lardner has the rookie outfielder describe his unfortunate debut against Johnson:

"They can't never tell me he throws them balls with his arm. He's got a gun concealed about his person and he shoots 'em up there. . . . I just tried to meet the first one he throwed, but when I stuck out my bat the catcher was throwing the pill back to Johnson. Then I thought: Maybe if I start swingin' now at the second one I'll hit the third one. So I let the second one come over and the ump guessed it was another strike, though I'll bet a thousand bucks he couldn't see it no more'n I could. While Johnson was still windin' up to pitch again I started to swing—and the big cuss crosses me with a slow one. I lunged at it twice and missed it both times. The Ath-a-letics was all laughin' at me and I laughed too, because I was glad that much of it was over."

That nobody ever threw a baseball as hard as Johnson was a self-evident proposition to all who saw him. Clinching the argument was the most interested of all parties—Walter himself. Before the reader jumps to the conclusion that this was the most prejudiced of all interested parties, too, remember that if there was anything about Johnson that overshadowed the speed with which he could throw a baseball it was his un-compromising honesty. He was his own severest critic. Yet sports writer Shirley Povich recalls the day he accompanied Walter to Washington's Griffith Stadium in 1941 to watch Bob Feller, then at his peak, pitch against the Senators.

"He's mighty fast," Johnson marveled as Feller cut down batter after batter with his blazing pitches.

Late in the game Povich put the question to Johnson. "Tell me, Walter, does Feller throw as hard as you did?"

Johnson was silent for fully three minutes. He screwed up his face and rubbed his chin and looked off into the distance. This was not a man figuring out a mathematical problem. Inside him there was going on a tremendous struggle between his modesty and his honesty. Honesty, of course, had to win out. Johnson looked at Povich, shook his head and said simply, "No."

This husky, blue-eyed country boy was exactly what the storybooks tell you a great athlete *should* be, but what he very seldom is. Though modest, Johnson had confidence in his prowess; though he was not prim, he attended church regularly, preferred checkers and casino to poker and did not like cigarettes, beer or whiskey; and though he was the most determined of competitors, he never deliberately used his peerless fast ball to intimidate an enemy hitter. The knockdown pitch and the beanball are as old as baseball itself and almost every big-league pitcher will tell you that hitters must be kept loose at the plate. But Johnson did not look at it that way. He would not risk injuring another player for the sake of winning a ball game.

Ty Cobb has admitted in recent years that he took advantage of Johnson's reluctance to throw at a hitter. "I guess I cheated some on Walter," Cobb says. "I knew that he was scared stiff of hitting a batter with his fast ball, so I used to crowd the plate. He'd see me hanging over it and he'd throw the ball outside and pretty soon he'd be behind on me. Then he'd have to let up a little and come in with a fat pitch and that was the only time I really could get my hits against him."

The story is told of the day a fast ball got away from Johnson and hit Eddie Collins on the leg. The brilliant second baseman fell to the ground and writhed in the dirt like a man in mortal agony. Walter, fearing that he had seriously injured Collins, rushed to his aid. After several minutes of what appeared to be excruciating pain, Collins climbed slowly to his feet and limped down to first base. With a "cripple" on base, Johnson did not hold him close to the bag and took his time while pitching to the next batter. On the first pitch, the "cripple" came to life and raced down to second base, stealing it easily.

Johnson was not upset because he had been duped by the shrewd Collins. His only comment was: "It was nice to know Eddie wasn't hurt."

There was a day in Boston when Johnson was locked in a tense pitchers' battle with the Red Sox. The two teams went into the the bottom of the ninth inning, still deadlocked at 0-0. With two out and a runner on first, the next batter slashed a hit up the middle of the diamond. The ball should have been fielded easily in center field and the batter held to a single, but Clyde Milan let it roll through his legs and the winning run scored from first base. Most pitchers would have berated their outfielder or, at best, eyed him for days in sullen silence. But, when Milan approached him afterward in the clubhouse to apologize, Walter merely shrugged and said, "That's all right,

Clyde. You don't do a thing like that very often. And besides, I should have struck the hitter out."

Vincent Flaherty tells of the day on which Johnson had his only dispute with an umpire. When he first came to the Senators he was so inexperienced that he had but the haziest idea of the game's rules. He knew that all he had to do to get enemy hitters out was to keep throwing his fast ball past them and that was enough to bring him to the big leagues. But on this particular day Walter came to bat and hit a long drive to left field. He rounded first and raced into second, well ahead of the outfielder's throw. Then, instead of stopping at the base, he kept right on running into short left field, just as he had always run past first. He walked slowly back to the base and was promptly tagged by the shortstop.

"You're out," the umpire said to Johnson.

Walter turned to him in disbelief. "Out?" he asked mildly. "But I got to second base a full step before the throw."

The umpire patiently explained to him that he was allowed to overrun first base, but not second.

"Excuse me, I'll remember that," Walter said, and walked off the field.

Like most great athletes, Johnson came from a poor family. Born on November 6, 1887, in Humboldt, Kansas, he passed his early years on his father's small farm there. In 1901 the family moved to the California oil fields, settling in Olinda, where the elder Johnson hoped to make his fortune. Although his father was to be disillusioned, Walter grew there into a powerful young man; he was six feet, two inches tall, weighed over two hundred pounds, had a ruddy, pleasing face and light brown curly hair. Having terrorized his schoolmates with his fast ball on the local sandlots, he entered professional baseball in 1906 and finally won a job with the Weiser, Idaho, club. Within a year, word of his fast ball had reached the big league scouts, he had been bought by the Senators and he was on his way to Washington.

On the whole those were dreary years for Washington's baseball fans, but there was always excitement in the ball park on afternoons when Johnson was pitching. The hum of his fast ball lured people to watch what was otherwise a drab team. To all exciting athletes accrue a number of nicknames and Johnson was no exception. "The Big Train is coming to town," Grantland Rice wrote of him once, and the name stuck; so did the name Barney, given him by a teammate because of Johnson's only vice, a boyish enthusiasm for fast automobiles, at a time when Barney Oldfield was the most famous racing driver in the country; and, not nearly so enduring, the name "Swede," given him because, though he was really of English, Dutch and Scotch-Irish descent, it was mistakenly assumed that he was Swedish. When a friend once asked him why he did not attempt to correct the mistake, Johnson shook his head.

"Oh, no, I wouldn't do that," he said. "The Swedes are mighty fine people and I don't want to do anything that might offend them."

It was hard to believe that such a kind, modest gentleman was capable of Johnson's incredible feats on the playing field. There was the time in 1908 that he shut out the Yankees in three straight games. Recalling the series years later, his face broke into a wide grin.

"They said I deserved a lot of credit for doing that," Walter said, "because the team needed me bad. But that wasn't the true story. I pitched against them on a Friday in early September and beat them, 3-0. I was sitting on the bench before the game the next day and a newspaperman went over to our manager, Joe Cantillon, and asked him who was going to pitch.

" 'Well, Johnson beat them yesterday,' Joe said, 'so I think I will pitch him again today.'

"That was the first I knew about it. I went out and pitched and shut them out again—I think the score was 6-0. There wasn't any Sunday baseball in New York then, but we were playing them a doubleheader on Monday. The newspaperman came down again before the first game and he asked Cantillon who was going to pitch. Joe leaned back and thought for a minute and then he said:

" 'Johnson's going good for us. I guess I'll pitch him again.'

"I shut them out 4-0 and my arm felt like it was about to fall off. When the game was over I went back into the clubhouse and I just kept out of sight of Cantillon. I stayed in the clubhouse until the players went on the field and I knew that the game had started. I was afraid that newspaperman was going to come down to the bench again and give Cantillon an idea."

There were other great moments. He struck out four Boston hitters in one inning in 1911, the fourth man getting a chance to bat when the Washington catcher dropped a third strike on a previous victim. In 1913 he pitched 56 consecutive scoreless innings. This was perhaps his greatest season, for he won 36 games while losing only 7, struck out 243 batters and walked only 38, and he had an earned run average of 1.14. In 1920 he pitched a no-hit, no-run game against Boston. He was not only the best pitcher in baseball, but the best hitting and fielding pitcher as well.

And all the while the Senators were also-rans. Johnson saw lesser pitchers, aided by fine ball clubs, compile impressive records and gain fame and gold in the World Series. And now

Johnson's chance seemed to have slipped by. The marvelous
right arm on which his greatness hung was beginning to wear
out. The Senators, under four different managers in the five
post-World War I years of 1919 through 1923, finished
seventh, sixth, fourth, sixth and fourth. They were the essence
of mediocrity. And then, in 1924, they came to life. Under a
new manager, Bucky Harris, the Senators smashed the Yankees' three-year reign in the American League and won the
pennant. Johnson, depending on his heart and his head rather
than his speed, played a big part in the victory by winning
twenty-three games. A country which had come to revere him
prayed that Johnson would enjoy the most satisfying triumph
a pitcher can know—victory in a World Series game.

As usual the odds were against Washington. The Senators
were the nation's sentimental favorites, but not the experts', for
their opponents were the resourceful New York Giants, playing in their fourth straight World Series. Led by the out-
rageously combative John McGraw, the Giants feared no
pitcher on earth, and certainly not a Walter Johnson who
seemed to have dipped well below his prime. The World
Series, of course, was a novelty in Washington, the first that
had ever been played there, and everybody in the city seemed
to want tickets. Many, evidently aware that Johnson found it
hard to say no, turned to him with their ticket problems. Gracious as always, Walter doled out $1,000 of his own money to
buy tickets for friends and acquaintances. For one reason or
another, many of these friends never bothered to pick up their
tickets from him or, picking them up, failed to pay him. That
World Series cost Johnson $360 before he threw a pitch.

Walter, as everybody had anticipated, was called on to open
the Series for the Senators. His opposing hurler was Arthur

Nehf, one of the toughest "clutch" pitchers of his day. Nehf was already an old hand at starting World Series games but Johnson, on the brink of this long-awaited adventure, felt as if he were a rookie once more.

Nehf was to say afterward to a friend, "Johnson was so nervous I felt sorry for him. I guess he knew that everybody was rooting for him. When we shook hands for the photographers before the game, his hand was trembling."

The game itself was the kind that sets the hardiest veteran to trembling. The Giants pecked away at Johnson, scoring in both the second and fourth innings, and kept him in trouble much of the time from there to the finish. Yet, just when it seemed that they must fall on him for a barrage of runs and drive him from the box, The Big Train would summon that wonderful fast ball out of the distant past and throw his way out of trouble. The Senators scored a run in the sixth and another in the ninth to send the game into extra innings. It was an extra burden on a man who was approaching his thirty-eighth birthday.

The Senators could not get the run that would have given Johnson his cherished victory. Nehf smothered their attack and, in the top of the twelfth inning, a walk, a bloop hit and a wild throw put Johnson in trouble; singles by Ross Youngs and Bill Terry blasted his dream. The two runs which the Giants picked up there insured their triumph, although the Senators got one of them back in the bottom of the inning. Johnson, in defeat, was magnificent, striking out twelve Giant hitters to tie what was then the Series record for a single game. But all of Washington and millions of fans around the country were saddened by his bitter defeat.

They were saddened, but not completely discouraged. The

grand veteran would surely get one more start in this World
Series. At the end of four games the teams had two victories
apiece and the Senators, having shaken off their earlier nervous-
ness, now felt that they had a good chance to upset the mighty
Giants. In an effort to move ahead, manager Harris selected
Johnson as his pitcher for the fifth game. But Walter, who at
one time had been able to pitch three shutouts in four days,
found now that the effort of going twelve innings five days
before had stripped him of the remnants of his fast ball. He
was rocked by thirteen hits, four of them by the Giants' rookie
third baseman, Freddie Lindstrom. His opposing pitcher, Jack
Bentley, clubbed him for a home run with a man on base in
the fifth inning, putting the Giants ahead, 3-1. And then,
when the Senators pared a run from that lead in the top of
the eighth, the Giants came right back in their half to score
three more times and put the game out of reach. The final
score was 6-2.

That seemed to have destroyed the dream of Walter Johnson. He would not get another start in the Series. But the
Senators battled back the next day and beat Nehf, 2-1, and a
seventh game was needed to decide the championship. Johnson
was on the bench as the game began. The Giants led, 3-1, after
seven innings, but Washington rallied for two runs in the last
of the eighth. During the rally Firpo Marberry, the Senators'
pitcher, had been removed for a pinch hitter and, as the Senators took the field for the ninth inning, a chant went up from
the stands. Over 31,000 people, including President Calvin
Coolidge, were there that day and every one of them wanted
to see Walter Johnson enter the game. Their wish came true.

When it had become apparent that Marberry would leave
the game for the pinch hitter, Harris had turned to Johnson

on the bench and had asked him if he would try to pitch an inning or two. Could this great pitcher, who had waited eighteen years to win his World Series game, do anything else but nod quietly and go down to the bullpen to warm up? He was sure his arm had a couple of good innings left.

The Giants were delighted at the arrival of a tired and aging pitcher on the mound. They were eager to wind up the game in the ninth. With one out, Frankie Frisch lined a triple to deep right center field. Here Harris came to the mound from his position at second base and ordered Johnson to walk the next batter, Ross Youngs. And now the Giants' cleanup hitter, George Kelly, was at the plate. A long fly would bring in the tie-breaking run.

The Giants never got the long fly they needed. As the crowd sat breathless in the stands, Johnson fired with all his old-time strength and Kelly struck out. Then Johnson retired Irish Meusel and one threat had been wiped out.

But the Senators failed to score in their half of the ninth and the rival teams entered extra innings. Johnson's, and Washington's, chances grew slimmer as each inning passed, for it seemed unlikely that this weary man could carry his burden much further. He got by the tenth inning without mishap, but Heinie Groh led off the eleventh for the Giants with a single and was sacrificed to second. The next batter was one of the most dangerous of all World Series competitors—Frisch. Johnson, remembering that ninth-inning triple, pitched brilliantly and Frisch went down on strikes. Again Youngs was given an intentional walk and again Johnson called on all his reserve speed and struck out Kelly.

There was no rest for the old man. The Senators were turned back once more in their half of the eleventh and the game went into the twelfth inning. Meusel opened the Giants' attack with a single. But Johnson refused to give up, refused to bow either to age or the Giants' powerful lineup. He struck out Hack Wilson and got past the next two New York hitters. And the Senators, desperately wanting to push across the winning run in this inning so that Johnson's agony would end, had another shot at Jack Bentley.

The first Washington hitter grounded out. Then Muddy Ruel lifted a high pop foul behind the plate. The Giants' veteran catcher, Hank Gowdy, tossed off his mask and went after it. And the incredible happened. Gowdy stepped into his mask. He frantically kicked it out of the way, set off after the ball again and once more stepped into the mask. His spikes caught in the mesh, he kicked furiously, finally freed himself, stumbled and saw the ball drop almost at his feet. Given another chance at bat, Ruel lined a double to left.

Every fan in the ball park felt that fortune was now turning in Johnson's favor. Walter, the next batter, received a tremendous ovation. He hit the ball on the ground to Travis Jackson, but the New York shortstop fumbled it and everybody was safe. Earl McNeely then hit another ground ball, this one directly at third baseman Lindstrom. Freddy went down for the ball, but he never touched it. The most famous pebble in baseball history was lying just in front of him. The ball hit the pebble, bounced high over Lindstrom's head into left field and Ruel raced home with the winning run.

Patience, a great heart and the shadow of a wonderful fast ball had rewarded Johnson for those eighteen years of frustration. He had his victory and it was the deciding game of the World Series, the only world championship that Washington has ever won. The Giants, beaten by a strange turn of fate, glumly boarded their train and rode back to New York. Suddenly Jack Bentley, the losing pitcher, broke the silence in the car.

"Cheer up, boys," he said. "It just looks like the Good Lord couldn't stand seeing Walter Johnson get beat again."

It might have been closer to the truth to say that the Good Lord was answering a million prayers.

Chapter 5 **The Cinderella Man**

If every American mother dreams that her son will grow up to become the President of the United States, there are surely millions of fathers who entertain at least once a fancy that their sons will grow sturdy and tall and win the heavyweight boxing championship of the world. In spite of all the abuse that this antiseptic age has heaped upon boxing, the man who wears the heavyweight crown still inspires almost universal respect. His is the loftiest position in the world of sports. Deep in every man there lies a chord which responds to the beery boast of that earliest of the great heavyweight champions, John L. Sullivan: "I can lick any man in the world!" The laughter of the coldest cynic can hardly chill the satisfaction that rises in a man when he has proven his right to make such a claim.

As John Lardner has pointed out in his book, *White Hopes and Other Tigers,* there have been periods in American history when the heavyweight champion outranked the President in public interest. "Jack Johnson's impact on popular feeling was sharper than William H. Taft's," Lardner wrote. "Jack Dempsey overshadowed Calvin Coolidge. Taft and Coolidge accepted the situation meekly, or, at any rate, with philosophy. Theirs were times of international peace and relaxation, when it seemed pure common sense to let human nature alone." Certainly the appeal of the great champions is understandable. Sullivan, the roaring bullyboy, came along at a time when the United States was flexing its own muscles as a world power, thrashed the English pretenders to his throne and seemed to embody the country's new international importance; Johnson irritated popular prejudices by climbing to the throne in those benighted days when it was considered somehow shameful that a Negro should rule the White Man's roost; Dempsey stirred what are commonly called the baser passions with the primitive savagery of his assaults; and Joe Louis, in a less benighted age, attracted a curious mixture of admiration and awe as the first widely accepted Negro athlete, and a fighter of extraordinary destructiveness.

All of those men were great champions. They dominated the heavyweight division in their own day. The record of James J. Braddock does not appear to place him on the same level with those illustrious fighters, for he won only 53 of his 84 professional bouts. After winning the heavyweight championship he did not fight again for over two years, and then lost the title the first time he tried to defend it. And yet Braddock occupies a prominent place in boxing history, and first place in the affections of millions of Americans. Like the others, he was a unique product of a specific era. His were not "times of international peace and relaxation." Braddock ascended to the title in the waning years of the Depression, having fallen from an earlier prosperity and then pulled himself out of the poverty and despair with which so many of his countrymen were only too familiar. "The Cinderella Man," they called him, and perhaps no other champion has been so real a national symbol.

Legend holds that Braddock's father, Joseph, came to this country on the same boat which carried the famous American heavyweight, Jake Kilrain, who returned after fighting a 106-round draw with Jem Smith in France. The year was 1889 and the elder Braddock, who was always proud of his Irish heritage, was coming, not from Ireland, but from England, where the family had been settled for many years. Braddock found work in New York City and moved into an apartment on West Forty-eighth Street, only a few blocks from where Madison Square Garden stands today. There the future champion was born in 1905 and christened James Walter Braddock. (The "James J." was an invention of his manager's, who reasoned that people would be more likely to remember the prefix made famous by such redoubtable battlers as James J. Corbett and James J. Jeffries.) The family moved to North Bergen, New Jersey, when Jim was a child. The young Braddock grew up there, impervious to the education directed at him by the good sisters in a neighboring parochial school, but remarkably susceptible to school-yard brawls. The Braddocks were a fighting family, possessing what is said to be the quick temper of their race, and a corresponding ability to handle themselves in an altercation of any sort. Jim's oldest brother, Joe, was an amateur fighter of some note in New Jersey, and Jim believed that his own informal experience in using his fists qualified him for a ring career, too.

Braddock was a natural fighter. He weighed about 160 pounds in his late teens, and he was a hard puncher and a tough and willing mixer. Boxing throughout his home state, and occasionally venturing into New York City, he took on all comers and beat many fighters far bigger than he was. He included among his amateur titles the middleweight and heavyweight championships of New Jersey. And then early in 1926 Braddock made the business connection and the lasting friendship that was to play so vital a role in his life.

Joe Gould was a talkative, clever and ambitious fight manager from New York City. Despite his youth, he had learned his lessons well in the murky world of boxing and he knew the angles which could push a sturdy young pug toward the top. He came to a gymnasium in Hoboken, New Jersey, one day to sell the contract of one of his fighters to a group of local bootleggers. The tentative price on the fighter, whose name was Harry Galfund, had been set at $2,500 and was to be shared by Gould and Galfund. The bootleggers, however, wanted to see the fighter in action first, and it was agreed that Galfund would box a few rounds in the gym.

"There is a tall kid shadowboxing up against the wall," Gould recalled years later, "and I ask him if he wants to make five bucks.

" 'Sure,' he says.

" 'All right,' I tell him. 'I just want you to box three rounds with this fellow over here.'

"Then I go back to Galfund, who was a pretty good fighter, and say, 'Now listen. Knock this bum out as quick as you can. Understand?'

"He says he does, but the bum kicks the tar out of him, and these bootleggers are all laughing at me. I finally have to settle with them for $1,200 and I give Galfund $600 and figure I am lucky to get off with that much. I find out that this bum's name is Braddock, and I give him ten dollars instead of five. When I find out that he needs a manager I arrange to handle him."

Braddock acquired a following in New Jersey soon after he became a professional. The fans liked this big, dark-haired kid with the crooked grin and the wallop in his right hand. He was approaching the light heavyweight limit of 175 pounds now, and he was beating some very good fighters. Then, in 1927, just when it seemed that Jim was about to move up as a contender for the light heavyweight championship, he broke his hand.

"He had to lay off for a few months," Gould said, "and as soon as he started training and hit somebody with that hand, it puffed up on him and we went to see a doctor about it. He said the hand had knit wrong and would have to be operated on, and he would do it for $1,500. We were broke so we went to see another doctor and he said he would do it for $1,200. Right after that I got a fight for Braddock with Paul Swiderski. Jim didn't dare do any boxing in training and when he got in the ring with Swiderski he threw his right hand at Paul's head, making sure to miss. He kept throwing his right all through the fight and missing with it on purpose, but it kept Swiderski at a distance and Jim managed to get a draw. As soon as we got the money for the fight we ran right to the doctor and he operated on the hand."

Jim then took advantage of the kind of break that every fighter needs in order to establish himself as a contender. Tuffy Griffiths, a terrific puncher, had built an impressive reputation for himself in the West, and he was matched with Pete Latzo in Madison Square Garden. Latzo, wanting a tune-up fight to prepare himself for his important match, took on Braddock in Newark. This was a mistake on Latzo's part. Braddock walloped Latzo so badly that Pete was unable to fight Griffiths in the Garden, and Braddock got the match instead. He went on to demolish Griffiths in two rounds, then earned a shot at the light heavyweight title by knocking out Jimmy Slattery.

He fought the champion, Tommy Loughran, at Yankee Stadium on July 18, 1929. What he and Gould had believed to be their big chance turned out to be instead the turning point in their fortunes. Loughran was one of the finest boxers the ring has known, and he easily handled the crude Braddock. Jim had only that good right hand in his favor and Loughran, sticking his left in the challenger's face and moving away from the deadly right, won the fifteen-round decision. It was a lesson that Braddock was to remember when his next big chance came to him six years later.

Seldom has a well-known athlete, of exceptional natural talent and still a healthy young man, plunged so abruptly toward oblivion. Surely he had not taken a physical beating from Loughran; the light-hitting champion's assault had been artistic rather than punishing. It was as if Braddock's determination, so fierce throughout his first three years in the ring, suddenly evaporated when he reached for, and missed, the championship. He had made an excellent try, but he had not been good enough, and now he seemed to have lost the compelling drive for success that is a part of every champion. Perhaps the title no longer seemed important to him. Fighting before big crowds at Madison Square Garden and Yankee Stadium, he had earned thousands of dollars, and his money, deposited in a bank and invested in a fleet of taxicabs, was apparently safe. And Jim was an easygoing fellow, who liked to join the boys for a few beers at the local speakeasy, and he was devoting much of his time to Mae Fox, the girl whom he married in 1930.

Braddock, of course, was a professional prize fighter, too, and once he climbed in the ring he fought with the unyielding courage which marked his entire career. A disheartening series of injuries contributed to his decline. His hands were a constant source of trouble, making it a torture to punch solidly and stripping him of his old knockout wallop. But whatever his injury, he never complained. He went through with one bout after suffering a severe shoulder injury in an automobile accident and losing the use of his right arm. Another time Gould had just finished giving him his instructions before the opening bell when Jim said to him, "I'll do the best I can, Joe, but don't expect too much of me."

"Why? What's the matter?" Gould asked.

"I got a busted rib," Braddock said matter-of-factly, and then went out and took a ten-round beating.

Soon all of the laughs began to go out of Jim Braddock's life. America was fast in the grip of the Depression, and he was among its early victims. His savings were wiped out when the bank in which he had deposited them collapsed. His fleet of taxis was also lost. Injuries kept him idle for long periods of time and, even when he was ready to fight, the report that he was washed up prevented him from getting bouts in which he could make any money. He was losing more often than he won. In the fall of 1932 he and Gould went to California looking for fights, and his luck took a turn for the worse. He won one of his first two bouts there, then suffered a deep cut over his eye in losing to Tom Patrick. Four stitches

were needed to close the wound. Only a few days later Gould
was asked by a San Francisco promoter if Braddock would
take the place of an ailing fighter against Lou Scozza. The cut
over Jim's eye had not healed but, after talking it over,
Braddock and Gould decided to accept the fight because they
needed the money. Scozza ripped open the cut in the early
rounds and, with Braddock bleeding badly, the referee stopped
the fight and awarded it to Scozza on a six-round knockout.

Braddock and Gould were wrong if they thought their
fortunes had finally hit bottom. Early in 1933 Braddock was
boxing in the big cities—New York, Philadelphia, Chicago
and St. Louis. By summer he was boxing on the small-town
circuit—Jersey City, West New York, New Jersey, and
Mount Vernon, New York. It was in Mount Vernon that
the career of the twenty-eight-year-old Braddock appeared to
have come to a dismal end. Accepting a bout with one Abe
Feldman despite an injured hand, Braddock gave an inept performance and the referee, exasperated by the former contender's inability to do any solid punching, stopped the fight
and declared it "no contest."

Only Gould had faith in Braddock now, and even his faith
was shaken. The friends that had once told Jim what a great
fellow he was and how he could always count on them now
shunned him. Promoters who once had bid for his services now
explained to Gould that there was no place for Braddock on
their fight cards. Jim and Mae moved their three children into
a smaller apartment in Woodcliff, New Jersey, and Jim turned
to the only job he knew outside of boxing—that of a dock
laborer. But work on the docks, just as it was everywhere,
was scarce, and there were some weeks when Braddock barely
earned twelve dollars.

Meanwhile, during that long winter of 1933-34, Gould kept looking and hoping. He haunted the offices of fight promoters, talking about Braddock so incessantly that even his friends grew tired of him. There was one bright moment when Gould got Jim a bout with the German heavyweight, Walter Neusel, in Brooklyn, but their excitement was brief. The state athletic commission refused to approve the match, deciding that Braddock was not a fit opponent for the highly regarded German. It was after that blow that Gould went to work selling appliances from door to door and gave part of his earnings to the stricken Braddock family.

Each morning Braddock awoke at six o'clock, put on his work clothes and walked three miles to the Weehawken piers, where he had a job unloading railroad ties from the ships that had brought them up from the South. It was back-breaking work, but it was building his body, putting him in better condition than he had ever known before. The Braddock who had weighed 175 pounds when he boxed Tommy Loughran in 1929 now was a husky and hard 195.

"The hard work helped to do that," Braddock said later, "but I guess all us Irishmen mature late, anyway. My uncle was a runner, and he told me once that he didn't hit his peak until he was forty years old."

But often there was no work to be found, hard or otherwise, and Braddock walked the streets for long hours. One evening he trudged home, opened the door, and found the tiny apartment in darkness.

"For God's sake, Mae, turn on the lights!" he called.

His wife came out of the gloom to meet him. "There aren't any lights, Jim," she said softly. "The electric company turned them off. And there's no gas, either."

Jim sat down heavily, wiping his face with a big hand. He was silent for a moment, then looked at Mae and said: "I guess that's it. The last thing in the world I want to do is go on relief. But the kids got to eat. We can't live like this. I'll go down and see about it in the morning."

Humiliated by having to appeal for help from the relief board, Braddock nevertheless saw no other choice before him. A friend who was in charge of local relief funds arranged for the Braddocks to receive help, and Jim supplemented the small relief check with whatever work he could find as a longshoreman. Gould scurried from one promoter's office to another, talking about Braddock, and sending Jim a few dollars here and there to meet a particularly pressing bill.

One afternoon in June, 1934, Gould was in the office of Jimmy Johnston, who then promoted the fights at Madison Square Garden. He was sitting on Johnston's desk, swinging his legs, making small talk with the fight mob and throwing Braddock's name into every conversation. Johnston was especially busy that afternoon because it was only a few days before the heavyweight championship fight between the huge Italian, Primo Carnera, who held the title, and Max Baer, the challenger. Baer was a big handsome kid from California who was regarded as the hardest puncher since Dempsey. His battering right hand had killed one man in the ring and reportedly brought about the death of another several weeks afterward. Carnera, whose only assets were his size and a group of gangster managers who had maneuvered him into the championship, had very little chance against Baer. His chances were further diminished by the beatings he was taking in camp every day from a young heavyweight named Corn Griffin. Griffin was a fine prospect and had taken the job as a sparring partner to gain experience and pick up some extra money. Johnston wanted to use him in a preliminary bout on the Carnera-Baer card, but he hadn't been able to find an opponent for him. The managers of all the likely heavyweights around had heard of his exploits in Carnera's camp and didn't want to risk their own fighters' reputations against a newcomer who was as yet unknown to the public.

"Have you got an opponent for Griffin yet?" Gould asked Johnston.

Johnston shook his head. "No. I'm still looking."

"Well, how about Braddock?" Gould said. "What's the matter with him? You keep telling me you'll use him if you find a spot."

A pained expression came over Johnston's face. "This is no match for Braddock to take, Joe. I'd like to help you, but this kid has been fighting regularly and he's been up there with Carnera getting in shape. Do you want to see Braddock get killed?"

"Give me the match, Jimmy," Gould pleaded. "Braddock can take care of himself."

Johnston shrugged. He liked Gould and he knew how desperately Braddock needed the money. He also needed an opponent for Griffin, and the fight was almost on top of him.

"Okay," he told Gould. "You got the match. I hope your man is ready."

Gould rushed to a telephone and called Braddock.

"I got you on the Baer-Carnera card," he told Jim, and he could sense the big fighter's excitement. "You only got two days to get ready. Can you make it?"

"Two days—two hours—what's the difference?" asked Braddock. "Hauling the railroad ties keeps a guy in shape."

Fifty-six thousand people were in the old Madison Square
Garden Bowl in Long Island City on June 14 to watch Baer
make his bid for the championship. The spectators who got to
their seats early saw a brawl that surpassed even most main
events in excitement. Young Corn Griffin, tanned and confident, walked into his veteran opponent and knocked him
down in the first round. Braddock climbed to his feet, tore
into Griffin and had the younger man hanging on at the bell.
In the second round Braddock hammered him all over the ring.
The crowd came to its feet, thrilled by the fury of Braddock's
attack. By the third round Griffin was defenseless and Braddock clubbed him to the floor and he was counted out.

"I did that on hash," Braddock said to Gould in the dressing
room. "Wait till you see what I can do on steaks."

Unfortunately, Braddock had hurt his hand again, and it
was not until November that he was able to return to the
ring. But this time Gould did not have to plead with Johnston
to use his fighter. The fans and the writers had been impressed
by Braddock's performance, and not even the fearful beating
which Baer had dealt Carnera to knock him out and win the
title had erased from their memories the sight of the hungry
and relentless Braddock. Johnston was anxious to get Braddock into action as soon as possible. Once again he found a
tough opponent for him—John Henry Lewis, who was to go
on to win the light heavyweight championship. But Braddock,
goaded by the desire to feed his family, had in him now the
old desire, and with it a mastery of his profession that he did
not have in his youth. He beat Lewis decisively, and suddenly
found himself once more an important figure in boxing.

The solitary advertising campaign which Gould had waged
on behalf of his fighter was about to pay rich dividends. They

made an appealing pair—Gould, the brash, clever and loyal little Jewish manager, and Braddock, the big, obedient, quiet, almost bashful Irish fighter. Gould knew that one more impressive victory could bring Braddock back to a point that, only a few months before, no one had believed possible. There were few serious contenders for Baer's title. Carnera, the ex-champion, had been exposed for the inept freak he was; Max Schmeling, another ex-champion, was fighting his way back into contention, although Baer had knocked him out before he beat Carnera; and Joe Louis, whose name was just beginning to appear in print, was at least a year away from consideration. The likeliest contenders at the moment were two young fighters named Art Lasky and Steve Hamas, but it was felt that each of them would have to gain one more victory over a reasonably good opponent before they would be attractive enough to the public to merit an outdoor fight with Baer.

This was where Braddock came in. He was matched with Lasky in a fifteen-round bout to be fought at the Garden on March 22, 1935. A convincing victory by Lasky would almost ensure him a shot at Baer's title in June. That Braddock was to be only a steppingstone in the rising career of Lasky was evident from the odds established by bookmakers before the fight; Jim was a 4-1 underdog. Then he went out and fought like a 1-10 favorite, using his left hand like a master and winning almost every round.

"He learned the hard way how to use that left hand," Gould said later. "His right hand has been hurt so much the last few years that Jim had to develop his left, or else get killed."

Braddock's first move after the fight was typical of him. He took part of his earnings and paid back to the local relief board the $300 he had received from them during the bleak period of his life when he was without work. Now his accounts had been squared.

And then it was as if all of the clouds in front of Braddock suddenly parted and gave him a glimpse of that pot of gold he had been chasing for so long. He had just eliminated Lasky as a contender; Schmeling did the same to Hamas, beating him badly in Germany; and Schmeling himself had made European commitments which would prevent him from fighting Baer in June.

"Who else is there but Braddock?" Gould, grinning broadly, asked the press. The New York State Athletic Commission, along with promoter Johnston, had to agree that there was nobody else. Braddock was named the number one contender and signed to fight Baer for the heavyweight championship in the Madison Square Garden Bowl on June 13, 1935.

"That's a big joke!" roared Baer's manager, Ancil Hoffman, when he learned that Braddock had been designated the leading contender. "I can take Max's kid brother Buddy back East and he could knock out Braddock. That guy won't draw flies in a title bout."

But, no matter how little chance Braddock was thought to have against the powerful Baer, the champion wanted to defend his title that year and Braddock was the only possible contender. Baer was a blustery fellow, essentially good natured, but given to posturing, clowning and assuming ferocious attitudes. There was plenty of ham in him (he was later to become a night-club comedian and a movie actor) and he knew how to play to the public. Baer announced that before he entered the ring he wanted to be assured that there would be an ambulance in attendance in case Braddock suffered serious injury at his hands.

Braddock, as challenger, occupied a curious position as the day of the fight approached. In a professional sense he did not merit a great deal of consideration. He had lost too many fights, had muffed too many opportunities, to seriously menace a champion whom many experts thought would eventually establish his greatness. The newspapers reported that he was a 10-1 underdog, and others suggested he was the poorest fighter ever to appear in a heavyweight title bout. On the other hand Braddock inspired an unprecedented wave of public sympathy and good will. The millions whose spirits and imaginations had been stifled by the Depression clutched at Braddock as a symbol. The papers, seizing on this fertile human-interest story, exploited Jim's dreary days on relief and his battle to feed a wife and three children. Who could root against a man fighting for his kids? The contrast between the close-mouthed, modest challenger and the braggart champion was also pointed out, and attracted many more fans to Braddock's side. The Irish, so proud of pugnaciousness in one of their own and badly in need of a real hero in those days, rallied to Braddock, as did those fans whose sympathies lie with the underdog no matter what the sport or the occasion.

Those who visited Braddock's training camp at Loch Sheldrake in the Catskill Mountains could not help but feel the unshakable confidence which filled the camp. Braddock and Gould were certain of victory, and so were most of the old-time boxing men who were in the camp as trainers, publicity men and just plain hangers-on. Gould had hired the toughest sparring partners he could find and Braddock found himself in a brawl almost every day. Sometimes he came out second best, but he was literally fighting himself into marvelous condition. He paid the price for it, too. He injured a rib so badly during one training session that he and Gould thought for a time that they might have to postpone the fight. But, padded with a leather protector, worn under two sweat shirts to conceal the injury from the writers, Jim went through his concluding workouts. The rib had partially healed by the night of the fight, but he entered the ring with a left arm so sore he could barely lift it.

The crowd of 30,000 at the arena was unquestionably behind Braddock, but there was about it at first a restraint which kept it from being especially noisy. Perhaps those who had come to see Braddock give the bullyboy a shellacking were secretly in dread that they would see instead their hero carted from the ring on his shield in the first round. That the odds against the challenger remained high was an indication his countless well-wishers did not dare to risk their money on his chances. At best, many of them placed small token bets. One newspaperman, converted by the overwhelming evidences of faith he had witnessed at Loch Sheldrake, scraped together and wagered $100 on Braddock at 8-1.

When the bout began it was clear that Braddock remembered the lesson he had learned the night he challenged Tommy Loughran for the light heavyweight title: two hands are better than one. Jim circled away from Baer's murderous right, sticking him with his left hand and, finding an occasional opening, banging him with his own right. In the third round Baer nailed him on the chin with a hard right. But Braddock, instead of retreating, piled into Baer and shook him up with a two-handed attack.

Braddock had taken the champion's best punch and it gave him new confidence. He was convinced now that Max had nothing with which to stop him. The crowd sensed this, too, and grew louder in its support. "Bang him one for the wife and kids, Jim!" a spectator would shout, and his neighbors, linked by the heartening conviction that they were doing their bit for a worthy cause, urged Braddock on. The way Jim outboxed Baer persuaded them that they were on the side of might, as well as right. Baer, frustrated by Braddock, took to posturing, wobbling his knees exaggeratedly when hit by the challenger, and making fierce faces and striking combative poses to disconcert him. But Jim just kept sticking his left in Baer's handsome face and evading that right hand. The noise increased in volume every round as Baer's chances waned. At the close of the fifteenth round the crowd was deliriously happy and Braddock's hand was raised in victory. It was the most startling boxing upset since Jim Corbett had knocked John L. Sullivan from his throne.

Jim's dressing room afforded visitors a view of what it must be like in a madhouse when the restrictions are off. The new champion sat on the rubbing table, unmarked except for a small cut on his nose and one on his left ear, grinning at the mob which surged around him. Gould, shouting and laughing, did as much jumping up and down as the crowd would allow him to.

"You fought a beautiful fight, Jim," one of his friends yelled at the champ. "My only complaint was you got hit with too many uppercuts in close."

"I know," Braddock grinned. "My left arm was so sore I couldn't get it up high enough to block them. I couldn't get any snap in my jabs either. All I could do was keep pushing my left hand into his face."

"And what are you going to do now, Champ?" somebody else asked.

"Well, the first thing I gotta do," Jim said, "is go out and try to buy some pet turtles. When I was leaving the house I told the kids I was going to bring home the title. They thought I meant a turtle, so I can't let them down."

And so began the most popular, if also the most uneventful, reign that any modern champion has had. It would be nice to say that Braddock lived happily ever after, but there hovered over that reign the specter of Joe Louis. It was obvious to everybody (except to Braddock himself) that he must eventually lose his title when he faced the magnificent young Negro fighter, but that did not detract from his popularity. Jim toured the country, fighting exhibitions and making appearances at banquets and charity affairs, winning new friends wherever he went. Louis' defeat by Schmeling, a long legal squabble among promoters and another broken hand suffered by Braddock in training kept him from defending his title for two years. When Jim was signed to meet Louis at Chicago on June 22, 1937, Gould was there to protect his interests. By signing the contract to fight under the promotion of Mike Jacobs (who had already obtained the exclusive rights to Louis' services) they automatically made Jacobs the dominant promoter in boxing. In return, Gould demanded, and got, a promise that he and Braddock would receive 10 per cent of the gate receipts from every heavyweight championship fight which Jacobs put on within the following ten years.

Braddock entered the fight with characteristic courage. If Louis thought that Jim would fall victim to the fright which had paralyzed most of his earlier opponents, he was mistaken. Braddock, taking the offensive in the first round, dropped the Brown Bomber with a left hook on the chin. It was one of the most dramatic moments boxing has known. For just a moment hope flared in the hearts of all those who admired the thirty-two-year-old champion. But Louis was not to be beaten. He climbed from the floor and began to bombard Braddock with his swift, deadly punches. By the sixth round the champion was nearly helpless. Louis hit him time and again with the blows that had demolished dozens of men before this, but Braddock remained on his feet. At the end of the round he reeled to his corner, terribly beaten, and flopped down on his stool.

"That's it, Jim," Gould said to him. "I'm going to have the referee stop the fight."

Braddock glared up at him through puffed eyes and muttered, "If you do, Joe, I'll never speak to you again."

Determined that, if he was going to lose, he would lose fighting in the center of the ring, not sitting on his stool, Braddock went out for the seventh round, and the slaughter continued. Somehow he survived that round, and went out on buckling legs for the eighth. A vicious series of punches sent him stumbling across the ring. Louis, following swiftly, measured him for one last punch, fired his right hand to the point of his chin, and Braddock went down on his back, unconscious. He had gone out as he had wanted to—as a champion.

Louis had begun the most impressive reign in the history of the heavyweight division, but boxing fans who lived through those years still look back on the time when Braddock was the champion, and they recall it as something special. Louis himself felt that Braddock was something special. With the honesty which marked all of Joe's public utterances, he called Braddock the bravest man he had ever fought, and whenever he met Jim he would always stick out his hand and say:

"Hello, Champ!"

Chapter 6 A Century's Quest

Glenn Cunningham, waiting for starter Johnny McHugh's gun to send him off on what he felt was to be the most important mile run of his career, fretted silently about his legs. It was not unusual. Scarred and fragile, they were a constant source of worry to him. The scars were a permanent reminder of that terrible morning in Kansas, so distant in his mind now it seemed that he had never been there himself, but that it had happened to somebody else.

And then the gun was fired and Cunningham shot forward. In his concentration on the race all other thoughts were swept away. He fell in behind Gene Venzke, the fine young miler from the University of Pennsylvania, letting him set the pace. Princeton's Bill Bonthron, the only other runner in this event, brought up the rear, but he was the man Cunningham feared. All through the winter season he and Bonthron had battled it out in the big mile races and Cunningham knew that if he was ever to assert his claim to recognition it would have to be done in this race.

It was June 16, 1934, and the big Reunion Day crowd at Princeton shouted encouragement to Bonthron. A bright sun shone down on the 25,000 people gathered in Palmer Stadium. The track, smooth and dry, promised a fast race. Cunningham felt a sharp twinge of pain in his right instep, injured in practice earlier in the week, as he took his first few steps, and then the pain was forgotten in the heat of the chase.

Venzke, running in that long rhythmic stride, set a good pace for the first quarter mile and Cunningham himself was clocked in 61.8 seconds. As they swung into the second quarter, Venzke slowed almost imperceptibly, harboring his strength for what he knew would be a grueling finish. But Cunningham felt like running now. He moved around Venzke, took the lead and pulled slowly away. Bonthron, not wanting to give his great rival a marked advantage, also passed Venzke and set out after Cunningham.

It was not until they had passed the half-mile mark that Bonthron sensed disaster. He was only seven yards behind the barrel-chested Kansas runner, who had completed the second quarter in 64 seconds. And then Cunningham opened up. Bonthron, at first, didn't know what to make of it. His rival seemed to have made his move a quarter of a mile too early. No man could keep up this pace. Cunningham pulled steadily away, building up his lead to ten yards, then twenty yards. Panicky, Bonthron stepped up his own pace, but he was not prepared for such speed at this point. The crowd, solidly behind Bonthron until now, suddenly stopped cheering. Cunningham had raced thirty yards in front and was still gaining.

Then the crowd knew it was in for a remarkable performance. The Kansan had run the third quarter in 61.8 seconds and was traveling even faster in the last quarter. Bonthron was already beaten, all the drive taken out of him by Cunningham's murderous pace. Coming down the final straightaway Glenn opened up a lead of forty yards over the man whom many had considered the finest miler in the world. As Glenn neared the tape the great crowd at Princeton stood to accord him a deafening ovation. Breaking the tape, he jogged on another thirty yards, then, still breathing heavily, turned and walked back to shake the hand of the weary Bonthron.

In a moment the news was being sent out over the world. After a long lapse the record for the mile had been returned to America, established by an amazing runner who had been, as a boy, a hopeless cripple. The new record was 4:06.7. It was a story that thrilled people wherever games are played.

It is not surprising that any symbol of man's power to push back the boundaries of his own capacity is treasured by most of us. In a world where teamwork and technology have, for good or evil, pointed the way, opportunities for any notable accomplishment by the individual body or mind are increasingly limited to the twin preserves of sport and art. "Everything that enlarges the sphere of human powers," Samuel Johnson wrote, "that shows man he can do what he thought he could not do, is valuable." The conquest of Mount Everest and the voyage of the raft *Kon-Tiki* stirred people everywhere because they were victories gained over nature with a minimum of technical assistance. The four-minute mile, which resisted for so long man's attempt to master it, was left as the most intriguing goal in the modern sports world.

It has been said that the four-minute mile was an arbitrary symbol, hit upon because "a mile" and "four minutes" are nice round numbers, but really possessing no more significance than any other distance and time one might designate. Yet we feel that the history of man's quest to break this barrier proves otherwise. Symbols, long established, tend to take on a reality of their own and, besides, there is no question now that its reality served as a formidable psychological obstacle for those who sought to conquer it. The mile is the most challenging and popular of all track events; here the speed of the sprinter must be combined with the endurance required of long-distance runners. And the first record for the mile having been established at four minutes and fifty-six seconds in 1864, the stage was set for the century-long assault on the four-minute mark.

It is surely a sign of our times that there were many men, including some who had devoted their lives to track, who were convinced that the four-minute mile was beyond the capacity of the human body. Brutus Hamilton, the University of California track coach who was one of the most influential men the sport has known, went so far as to compute, with the aid of charts and graphs, that the "dream" mile was beyond human endurance. Hamilton revealed, in the late 1930's, that the fastest possible time in which a man could run a mile was 4:01.66. At about the same time Jake Weber, a famous track coach at Fordham, came to the same conclusion without the aid of charts and figures. Basing his prediction on his own experience as coach and trainer, he said, "There will never be a four-minute mile. A man's heart will not stand it, and that's all there is to it. Perhaps some one may be able to get down to

4:03, but not a fraction of a second lower. Four minutes is absolutely a physical impossibility."

The story of the four-minute mile had an unpromising beginning, and its development was agonizingly slow. An Englishman named Charles Lawes was clocked at 4:56 in 1864, but a series of his determined countrymen got the mark down to 4:18.4 within twenty years. After that the seconds were lopped off considerably more slowly. By the First World War the record, held by an American named Norman Taber, stood at 4:12.6, and the emphasis in the mile run still lay on winning races rather than setting records. The runners' strategy was to rely on conservative pace-setting and jockeying for position, then to try to steal the race with a fast finish.

The world of track probably became time conscious after the First World War with the appearance of the magnificent Finnish runner, Paavo Nurmi. Nurmi ran with a stop watch strapped to his wrist. He claimed that he ignored his competition in a race and ran only "against the watch," keeping pace with a schedule he had set for himself in advance. Some later runners have laughed at Nurmi's eccentricity, arguing that he couldn't possibly have checked a stop watch while running at top speed but, whatever the explanation, Nurmi and his traveling clock made the public aware of time and records. When, in 1923, Nurmi lowered the mark to 4:10.4, people began to get excited about the possibility of a four-minute mile.

The great effort was on. If it was finally to be done it would require endurance, persistence and courage. Men would have to keep pushing themselves to faster and faster speeds over the grueling distance of the mile, increasing their capacity by untold hours of dogged practice runs. And, when the record was at last approached, there was the additional psychological hazard that no one really knew whether the body could stand up under such a pace. Perhaps the skeptics were right and the heart would give out at the critical moment.

For Americans the most fascinating parts of the story are built around two men—Cunningham, the Kansan who dominated American mile races during the 1930's and who made the first approach to the record in this country, and Roger Bannister, the young English doctor who brought the quest to its climax. As Bannister realized perhaps most vividly of all, no single man is deserving of all the credit for this accomplishment. Many men carried the burden, moving it closer and closer to the goal. Bannister, at the threshold, seized it and carried it across.

Cunningham, to many followers of sports, typified the determination of the runners in pursuit of the dream mile. He grew up in the town of Elkhart, Kansas, the son of a farmer. At seven he was attending the little school in town, and he and his older brother, Floyd, used to run to the schoolhouse in the mornings after completing their chores at home. A minor chore always lay before them at school. They were paid a few cents a week to light the kerosene stove so that the classroom would be warm when the other children arrived.

One morning in 1916 he and Floyd rushed into the classroom, picked up what they thought was the kerosene and poured it into the stove. The room became an inferno. Someone had accidentally left a can of gasoline by the stove. Little Glenn lost consciousness for a moment, then stumbled out into the snow. He looked around for Floyd, but his brother had not come out. Hearing screams from the schoolhouse, he rushed back, blindly fighting his way through the smoke and flame. His stockings and trousers caught fire and the flames flared up about him. He lost consciousness again.

When he awoke he was in his bed at home, his body swathed in oil bandages. The pain in his legs was intense. Floyd had perished in the fire and for a time the doctors had believed that Glenn would follow his older brother in death. Now, although it appeared his chances for survival were good, the doctors feared that he would never walk again. His left foot had been so badly burned the transverse arch was destroyed and he nearly lost his leg. His right leg had been shriveled and drawn up by scar tissue, leaving it several inches shorter than the other. A life as a cripple faced the little fellow who had loved to run across the Kansas plains.

And now there appeared in Glenn the determination that was to mark his career as an athlete. He hobbled around the house on crutches for almost three years, growing more agile on them and testing his legs as often as he could stand the pain. At night his mother and father massaged his legs for hours and, when they had gone to bed, Glenn sat up and massaged them himself. When he was ten years old he discarded his crutches and learned to walk painfully on legs still made stiff by scar tissue.

"I finally figured out," Glenn has recalled, "that if I ran or sort of hippety-hopped along I would concentrate so much on what I was doing that I'd forget the pain."

He ran wherever he went. His legs slowly began to straighten out and, even more slowly, the pain left them. At twelve he still limped, but he had a job in a granary and he could play with the other boys in Elkhart. There was only one sport for a boy to whom running meant so much. At first the longer races were too much for him and he competed in sprints, developing his speed and sharpening his reflexes. But there was in him an urge to run farther and he found that the mile races suited him better. As a junior he made the high school track team and was almost immediately a star. He had beaten his frightful burns. Now he was not satisfied merely to be a competitor. He wanted to be an outstanding one.

Brutus Hamilton, then the track coach at the University of Kansas, saw Cunningham in several high school meets and arranged for him to receive a scholarship to Kansas. "He could become the greatest miler America has ever had," Hamilton said of the barrel-chested young man. He was a lot closer to being right then than in later years when he computed man's inability to run the four-minute mile. In 1931, Cunningham's sophomore year at Kansas, a Frenchman named Jules Ladoumegue shattered Nurmi's record, running the mile in 4:09.2 at Paris. Not long afterward Glenn made himself known outside of his native state by winning the NCAA mile and setting a new American record with a time of 4:11.1.

As the seconds were knocked off the record, slowly closing the gap between it and four minutes, interest in the dream mile extended beyond the track world. And, just as people who care nothing for baseball become aroused at the mention of Babe Ruth's record of sixty home runs, and as those who wouldn't walk across the street to see a horse race on any other day of the year suddenly show a lively interest in the Kentucky Derby, so there were millions of people intrigued by the challenge of the four-minute mile. Sportswriters, on rainy days with nothing else to write about, could turn to the dream mile as an old friend and speculate on it for the length of their columns; it not only filled up space, but people were eager to read about it, too. The emergence of Cunningham served to stimulate interest in the mile in the United States. He was a remarkable young runner, he had fought his way back from a cripple's bed and he was certain to lower the record still further.

Cunningham's triumphs began to mount. He was selected for the United States Olympic team in 1932 and finished fourth in the 1,500-meter race ("the metric mile") at the Olympics in Los Angeles. In 1933 he was awarded the Sullivan Trophy, given each year to America's outstanding amateur athlete. And, important to Cunningham, too, was his selection as the honor man of the class of 1934 at Kansas, a tribute paid to him because of his fine academic record, his student activities and his service to the university. He was now the finest miler in the country, challenged only by Princeton's Bill Bonthron. New Zealand's Jack Lovelock, running in a meet at Princeton in 1933, had lowered the world record to 4:07.6. Matched in the same meet a year later, Cunningham and Bonthron hoped to approach that mark. Glenn looked forward to the race as a test; he and Bonthron had been trading victories in track meets until then. Cunningham felt that, if he were ever to move on to greatness, he must pull away from his competitors now. He was reaching the peak of his career.

The 25,000 people who saw that race at Princeton in 1934 will never forget it. That was Cunningham's finest race. By his blazing finish he had smashed the world record, bringing it down to 4:06.7. That mark was to stand until 1937 and no one was to knock more than a half second from it for eight years. He had also established his claim to the title of the world's best miler.

He was running in a unique atmosphere now. The fans

paid their money not so much to see exciting races but to be present at the setting of new records. Time, not victory, was the chief objective of the leading milers. While Cunningham dominated the field for the rest of the decade he seemed to have run the mile as fast as he possibly could. Sydney Wooderson of England lowered the record by .3 of a second in 1937, but the drive on the four-minute mark had apparently bogged down. Perhaps the skeptics were right and the human body had not been designed to withstand such pressure. Then Cunningham made one more try at it. In 1938 he went to Dartmouth and, on the new track there, ran a mile in which he was "paced" by Dartmouth runners. After leading him by running as fast as possible, each man dropped out in turn and Glenn finally drove himself to an astounding mark of 4:04.4. Because it had not been a race in the usual sense, however, the time was not recognized as authentic by any of track's ruling bodies. The record, 4:06.4, remained in Wooderson's possession and, when Cunningham finally retired in 1940, man was no nearer to the dream mile.

Glenn, however, by his consistently fast times (until then 4:10 had been reached only thirty-one times, twelve by Cunningham), had set a pace which increased the standards for milers everywhere. Though his 4:04.4 at Dartmouth was not recognized by the pooh-bahs of the sport, it demonstrated that several seconds could be shaved from the existing record under the proper conditions. Hampered by bad legs throughout his career, Cunningham has served as a model for the persistence and durability which would be required of the great milers of the future.

The start of World War II stifled the development of athletes in most of Europe and America. Only in Sweden, one of the few neutral nations, was the sport able to make significant strides. There two runners, Gunder Haegg and Arne Andersson, took turns breaking the record for the mile so that at the end of the war it stood at 4:01.4, a mark set by Haegg in 1945. The Swedes had come so close that all skepticism had been dispelled. It was obvious that the goal was now within reach and many believed the first four-minute miler would appear in the tremendous sporting resurgence immediately after peace had been restored.

Once again there was a curious lull, as if the milers were gathering their strength for the one superb effort which would carry them over the top. Nineteen fifty passed and no one had been able to surpass Haegg's mark. Then in 1951 there appeared in this country a young Englishman named Roger Bannister. Running in the Penn relays against some of America's finest milers, Bannister won off by himself in 4:08.3. Because he was only twenty-two years old and had had little experience against the finest competition, his time was considered remarkable. Veteran trackmen at the meet were forcibly impressed by him.

"He could be the greatest miler of them all," Asa Bushnell, a well-known official, said. "He's young, strong and fast. There's no telling what he can do."

Another official there was equally enthusiastic. "Bannister is the one man I've seen who I think is capable of running the four-minute mile. There was a slow pace out there today and the track was very soft. Right now he can do much better than he did today. And he'll get better as time goes by."

Bannister was the true amateur, a boy who grew up during the war years in England and found in running a wild sense of elation. His primary interest was medicine but when he entered Oxford University in 1946 he saw running as the ideal recreation with which to break up the grueling hours of study. Nobody paid much attention to the slender blond boy until the spring of 1947. Then he was chosen as one of the Oxford runners who would compete against Cambridge in a mile race. Trailing for most of the mile, he was suddenly overcome by the urge to push himself beyond what he had ever attempted before. In a terrific finish he raced past the leaders and won the race. His time was 4:30.8, but he had proved to himself he could win on the university level. He found something else, too. In his autobiography, published by Dodd, Mead & Co. in 1958, Bannister looked back to that race:

"I had expressed something of my attitude to life in the only way it could be expressed, and it was this that gave me the thrill. It was intensity of living, joy in struggle, freedom in toil, satisfaction at the mental and physical cost. It gave me a glimpse of the future because I had discovered my gift for running—an unconscious conspiracy of mind and body that made this energy release possible. I knew from that day that I could develop this newly found ability."

Later Bannister came to look on running as more than just a personal affair; intensely patriotic, he believed that by his running he could add to his country's prestige. He also saw the essential camaraderie in track and field events and realized that individual athletes could help each other in competition, a point that was to prove crucial in his progress later on. Meanwhile he was becoming one of England's best-known runners. For a time he competed in half-mile races. These had the same effect on him as the sprints had had on Cunningham—they helped him to develop his speed and reflexes. Chosen for the 1952 Olympic team after his brilliant showing on the

American tour the year before, Bannister looked forward with confidence to winning the 1,500-meter race, the Olympics' version of the mile. He had worked out a system of training which he believed would bring him up to the Olympic finals at the peak of his form. Feeling that he was hurt by too much work, he tempered his training, then registered such exceptional times in trial runs that he was confident of bringing victory to England.

His hopes were dashed several days before the big race in Helsinki, Finland. Having looked forward to a day of rest between the qualifying heats and the finals, he suddenly learned that the Olympic officials had decided to schedule three straight days of races—the heats, the semifinals and the finals. Bannister's training had not prepared him for such a grueling struggle. He made it to the finals, then had nothing left for his finishing burst. He finished fourth.

He felt that he had let his country down, and he realized that he had counted too heavily on one event. Nevertheless, his joy in running had not diminished and now there lay before him an even greater challenge—one that, if he could meet it, would bring more glory to England than an Olympic victory. After a long period when no one had threatened the four-minute mile, world-wide excitement had been stirred by the feats of a young Australian runner named John Landy. Landy had run several miles in better than 4:03, the fastest times since Haegg and Andersson had been at their peak during the war years. Bannister's times in the practice runs for his Olympic performance had convinced him that he could approach the four-minute mile with just a minimum of improvement. He now drove himself to gain the added speed and endurance which could bring him the ultimate success.

Bannister was battling time on several levels. Not only must he lower his running time, but he must get it down before Landy reached the same point. Here Roger enlisted the aid of several of his friends who were also runners. Men like Chris Chataway helped to set a furious pace for him on the track, goading him to greater efforts. He ran a 4:03.6 mile in the spring of 1953. Now another threat to Bannister's dream appeared. An American runner, Wes Santee, proved that the four-minute mile was within his reach, too. Fearful that Santee or Landy would get there first, Bannister ran a "paced" mile in June of that year and got his time down to 4:02. While one runner paced him through the early part of the race, another, Chris Brasher, slowed down so that he ran only two laps while the others were running three. Then, when Bannister had almost lapped him, the well-rested Brasher put on a spurt through the last quarter and Bannister tried to catch him. This produced a near-record time but, because of the conditions under which the race had been run, it was not considered a valid attempt.

Bannister, too, did not want to break the mark in a "race" of that kind. He looked forward to running the four-minute mile under competition. Throughout the winter of 1953-54 Bannister and Brasher worked on their speed and endurance by racing quarter miles, trying to bring their time down. A few weeks of mountain climbing in Scotland also built up their endurance. By the spring Bannister felt he was ready.

The date was May 6, 1954. Bannister had entered a race at Oxford and he had determined that he would make his try that day. He could not afford to wait any longer. Both Landy and Santee were entered in big races in Finland and the United States, respectively, in the coming weeks and there was a good chance that one of them would run the dream mile. The weather at Oxford, windy and overcast, was not ideal for the attempt, but Bannister had made up his mind. He had once defined the secret of running the four-minute mile: "It's the ability to take more out of yourself than you've got." He would now have the opportunity to demonstrate his theory.

Brasher moved away in front, setting an ideal pace for his friend. They reached the first quarter in 57.5 and the half in 1:58.2. This was on schedule, for Bannister knew that he would have to run the first half in less than two minutes. Now Brasher dropped back and Chataway took over the lead. This was the third lap, the one in which Bannister must hoard his strength for the final drive and yet keep close enough to the pace to bring the mark within his reach. They passed the three-quarter point in 3:00.5 and then Bannister went to the front at the beginning of the back straight and he was on his own.

There was a fire in his heels now. It seemed to him that he had nothing left for his last effort, but he dug down within himself and he found the strength to go on. The years of training, the confidence that had slowly mounted in him and the great pride in himself and his country drove him on. "I didn't think I'd make it," he said later. "As I came up to the tape it seemed to recede."

Bannister crossed the finish line and collapsed. He had taken out of himself more than he had to give, but the effort had not been in vain. When the announcer said the words: "The time, three minutes . . ." a great roar came from the crowd, drowning out the rest of the phrase and testifying to the spectators' immense pride in the achievement of the young Briton. The official time was 3:59.4.

That the attainment of the four-minute mile was more than just a triumph for Bannister's speed and endurance was proved by subsequent events. Six weeks later Landy, running against Chataway in Finland, lowered the record to 3:58. In August Bannister and Landy met in "The Mile of the Century" at Vancouver, Canada, and both finished the race in less than four minutes. Bannister, with a stirring spurt in the final yards, overtook Landy to win in 3:58.5. The Australian, finishing five yards behind, was timed in 3:59.6. The gates had been opened and the four-minute mile became almost commonplace. In a race at Dublin in the summer of 1958 five runners finished the mile in less than four minutes.

By believing in himself, pushing himself to his farthest limits and proving to others that the human body could accomplish what had once seemed far beyond it, the tall Englishman had wiped out that imposing psychological barrier. Others since have run the mile faster than Bannister, but that does not obscure his triumph; others circled the globe in faster time than Magellan after he had demonstrated to everybody's satisfaction that it was round. Roger Bannister will be remembered as one of the pioneers of sport, for he led the way where no one had been before.

Chapter 7 **Queen Helen**

There was a small crowd in the stadium at Forest Hills that afternoon in 1933. Four days of rain had dampened the enthusiasm of tennis fans for what had seemed, even in the first place, a cut-and-dried finals of the Women's National Singles championship. The great Helen Wills, who had lost only two *sets*, and not a single match, in seven years, was playing Helen Jacobs, a girl whom she had had little difficulty in beating in the past. What interest there was in the outcome of the finals centered on a reputed feud between the two Helens (both natives of Berkeley, California), and the back trouble which had kept Miss Wills from playing in the Wightman Cup matches only a couple of weeks before.

These points were hardly tangible enough to lure a big crowd to Forest Hills. Helen Wills had repeatedly denied the story of a feud with the other girl and then she had seemed to dispel any fears about the condition of her back by blasting her way through the championship tournament until she had reached the finals. There had been several lapses in the early rounds, but there had also been flashes of the skill that had enabled her to win the championship seven times before.

Then the match got under way and Miss Wills' fans were not so sure of their favorite's chances. Miss Jacobs, playing a bold game, seemed to share none of the awe felt by most women when they walked on the court against "Queen Helen." Miss Wills obviously lacked both the speed and the power she had always shown at the top of her form. Miss Jacobs, playing steadily, won the long first set, 8-6. Suddenly the older woman began to battle back. She asserted once more her superiority over the stockily built Miss Jacobs and won the second set decisively, 6-3. The crowd settled back to watch her take her opponent apart in the deciding set.

But Helen Wills had gone as far as she could. Miss Jacobs again took command and, before the crowd knew what was happening, jumped off to a 3-0 lead. The younger woman was on the verge of the most satisfying triumph of her career —a clear-cut victory over her arch rival. Even Miss Wills' supporters in the crowd seemed happy that, after their heroine's long list of triumphs, she would finally give way to the girl who had battled so long for this moment.

And then a startling thing happened. As Miss Jacobs was about to serve, Queen Helen turned away and walked over to the umpire. She said a few words to him, then leaned over and picked up her blue sweater and began to put it on. Miss Jacobs rushed over to find out what was going on. Suddenly the crowd let out a groan of anger and disappointment. Helen

Wills, about to go down to defeat, was walking off the court instead. The championship went to Helen Jacobs, but it was a hollow triumph for her.

There began an uproar whose intensity was almost unprecedented in the staid old game of tennis. The mob, which never lets pass a chance to jump on a champion who has faltered, heaped its criticism on Helen Wills. The most celebrated woman athlete of her time had quit in the middle of a championship match, robbing Helen Jacobs of the chance to win the title as a champion should. The explanation by Miss Wills' friends that she had injured her back was hooted down.

It is hard for us at this distance to imagine the furor which could arise over a back pain suffered by a woman tennis player. In most cases the abrupt retirement from play by a lady would occasion only a few remarks to the effect that all women are obviously peculiar and, anyway, a lady has a right to change her mind. But this was not "most cases." This was a case involving Helen Wills, a remarkable athlete and a remarkable woman. Those who knew her were aware that the story had not ended there at Forest Hills.

There was never anything ordinary about Helen. As a little girl she loved all games that could be played outdoors. It wasn't until 1919, however, that she got her first chance to play tennis. Her father, who had just returned to their home in California after World War I, liked tennis and decided to teach his daughter to play. In a few weeks this pretty thirteen-year-old girl with the long pigtails and unlimited energy was soundly beating her father. The blow to his vanity was to be softened by his daughter's later triumphs.

There were no obstacles for her on the way to stardom. The courts at the Berkeley Tennis Club were good, and her father saw that she received the finest coaching. Pretty soon she had run out of opponents there among the girls her age and she began to take on the men and boys at the club. Playing their hard-hitting game she developed rapidly, learning to cover ground and acquiring some powerful shots of her own. In 1921, when she was fifteen, Helen won the Pacific Coast Junior Girls' Championship, then was chosen to represent California in the National Junior Girls' Championship at Forest Hills, New York. There, in the big stadium that is the capital of United States tennis, Helen caught the fancy of the crowd with her flying pigtails and the white eyeshade that was to become her trademark. It wasn't long before she had caught everybody's fancy with her tennis, too. She beat an experienced eighteen-year old girl in the opening round and then went on to win the championship.

The next year she jumped into competition against the top players in America and finally surprised everybody by going all the way to the finals of the National Singles before losing out to the celebrated Molla Mallory, who had already won the championship five times. Obviously it was not going to be long before young Miss Wills ruled the roost. Nineteen twenty-three was her year. She dethroned Mrs. Mallory for the national title and then was selected to play on the Wightman Cup team against England. A year later she won the Olympics' singles and doubles championships; since tennis was taken from the list of Olympic sports after that year, Helen still reigns as the women's Olympic champion.

This was "The Golden Age of Sport" in America, an era that was dotted with tremendous names—Babe Ruth, Jack Dempsey, Earl Sande, Bobby Jones, Bill Tilden and Red Grange. The name of Helen Wills will always be included in this list of athletes who quickened the pulse of an entire decade. She dominated women's tennis as the others dominated their sports, and she was still "Queen Helen" when the others had passed from the scene. The white eyeshade, lined in green, became one of the symbols of that era; thousands of people went to play tennis wearing similar eyeshades. Just as famous was a nickname given her by the sports writers: "Little Miss Poker Face," they called her. She destroyed her opponents on the tennis court with as little visible emotion as Joe Louis was to show as he terrorized the heavyweight division a decade later.

Certainly she was not an uninspired player. She had tremendous determination, a will to win which some sports writers compared with Dempsey's "killer instinct." Her stolid expression during her matches was undoubtedly due to the quality she prized above all others in a tennis player—concentration. This strong-willed woman was able to discipline her mind so that everything which did not bear directly on the match at hand was excluded from her attention. She was seldom subject to the distractions or petty annoyances which can so completely upset most players that they go to pieces at a crucial moment.

And so, with her concentration, her stamina, her power and her fine assortment of shots, Helen Wills became the best woman tennis player in the world. At Wimbledon, Forest Hills or wherever else she played she so dominated her opponents that she invariably won in straight sets. A talented woman who was an excellent painter in her hours away from the courts, Helen attracted the admiration of European royalty; she was presented to the Queen of England at Buckingham Palace and she played tennis with King Gustave of Sweden. She numbered famous writers and artists among her friends. Her popularity was perhaps greater in Europe than it was in the United States.

As the 1933 season got under way there was no hint that Helen was in for trouble. Having climbed to the top in her teens, she was still comparatively young, despite her long reign; she was just twenty-seven. Yet Helen herself knew that she was not "right." She had strained her back early in the year and all the usual remedies had failed to relieve her pain. At Wimbledon she was able to conserve her energy, playing a conservative game, and still walk off the court with the championship. But, by the time she returned to the United States for the summer season, her back was worse than ever.

"The pain was everywhere," she was to write later in her autobiography, "down my back and leg and into the toes of my right foot. My right leg didn't do as it was told, because it seemed numb."

Although she wanted very much to play in the Wightman Cup matches, she was advised by her doctor to rest. The medical diagnosis was that she was suffering with "sub-acute unstable fifth lumbar vertebra symptoms." Whatever the explanation, Helen was in pain. She was also advised to pass up the Nationals at Forest Hills, but here the competitor in her rose to the surface and she insisted on playing.

"It may be my last chance to play at Forest Hills," Helen, already thinking of retirement, said. "I think I can make it."

In the opening rounds of the tournament she played well below her usual form, substituting guile for her renowned power. Then, in the third round, she seemed to find herself. Matched against a leading English player, Mrs. L. R. C. Mitchell, she gave an overwhelming performance to win, 6-1, 6-2. The *New York Times* was impressed: "It was by far the most

withering onslaught so far let loose in the tournament," its
account of the match read.

The doubts returned during the semifinals, in which Helen
lost a set in the United States for the first time since 1926. That
in itself was headline news. England's Betty Nuthall was her
opponent, and Miss Nuthall won the opening set, 6-2. During
the second set the excitement became so intense that Helen
served in two straight games, a violation which was overlooked
by both the players and the officials. It was the first time such
a mix-up had ever occurred in a championship match in this
country. Whether this led to the Englishwoman's defeat is a
question that no one could answer. As it was, Helen went on
to take the next two sets, 6-3 and 6-2, and enter the finals.

"I guess the officials will have to watch me more closely,"
was Helen's reply to questions about the mix-up.

Four days of rain interrupted the tournament at this point.
When the finals eventually did take place, Helen's back was
worse than ever. Nevertheless she kept it a secret from the
public, hoping that she could battle through one more match.
Her opponent in the finals, Helen Jacobs, was in questionable
condition too; she had fainted after a recent tournament, an
attack which had been brought on by gall bladder trouble.

Although the two girls were products of the Berkeley Tennis
Club, they were not especially close friends off the court and
this inevitably gave rise to rumors of a feud between them.
Miss Wills insisted that there was no feud of any kind; she
was older and her interests were different than those of Miss
Jacobs. Nevertheless, this meeting had been built up as a
grudge match.

Miss Jacobs, sensing that her opponent was not at her best,
took the initiative right from the start and won the first set,

8-6. Rallying to win the second set, 6-3, Miss Wills evidently pushed herself to the limit. When she walked off the court for the brief rest between the second and third sets she already looked like a beaten player. A friend who looked in on her in the dressing room was shocked by what she saw.

"Helen was lying on a couch," the friend said, "and she looked as spent as anyone could possibly be. Her color was almost frightening, and there were deep, heavy circles under her eyes."

Miss Wills was persuaded to take some aromatic spirits of ammonia as a stimulant and then she went out to the center court for the final set. She never had a chance. Miss Jacobs, playing steadily, quickly wore her down. "Then everything began to spin before my eyes," Miss Wills said later. "I felt as if I were going to faint because of the pain in my back and hip. My leg was completely numb."

The controversy began to rage as soon as she walked off the court. "Thank God our women players aren't urged to keep playing until they drop unconscious," was how her defenders put it. Others, blood brothers of the fans who boo the referee when he prevents manslaughter in the ring by stopping a one-sided fight, thought Miss Wills should have been carried off on her shield. "That's the way real champions go out," said people who howl for the doctor whenever they cut themselves shaving. Other critics of the beaten woman were quick to point out that she had failed to shake hands with her conqueror before going off the court. The stories of a feud between the two Berkeley girls was hotter than ever.

Helen Wills, herself, brooded about the uproar her action had caused. "I feel I've spoiled the finish of the National Championships," she said. "I wish I'd followed my doctor's advice and gone home to California."

She went home to California, all right, but she was determined to come back. All thoughts about her early retirement were pushed aside now. Her courage, her sportsmanship, had been doubted. The biggest match of her career lay ahead of her.

It was a long struggle. First there was a month in the hospital as the doctors tried to correct the injury. Then there was a lengthy convalescence. When Helen was well enough to get around normally again, her father, a doctor himself, advised that she build up her body by swimming every day. Helen did not play tennis during the rest of 1933, nor for all of 1934. It was only in the early days of 1935 that she felt well enough to pick up a racquet and go on the court again. Her injury had been more serious than anyone had realized.

Now Helen began to understand the difficulty of a comeback. Naturally cautious at first because of the possibility of reinjuring her back, she struggled to regain her co-ordination and her once-marvelous physical condition. Her many hours in the swimming pool had helped to tone her muscles and make her return to an active schedule that much easier. Slowly the strength and resiliency returned to her arms and legs.

Suddenly it was May and Helen knew that she wanted to play in one more big tournament, and that one was the biggest of all—Wimbledon. She needed more practice and she would have to increase her running speed if she was to cover the court properly against the better women players, but she felt that this was the moment to make her bid. She sailed for England.

Things did not go well for her after her arrival. A great deal of rain cut down on the time she had planned to have in actual competition in several of England's minor tournaments. And, while her stamina and co-ordination satisfied her, she was not able to get about the court as nimbly as she would have liked. In the days leading up to the opening of the tournament she practiced running by herself: first crouching, then suddenly spurting ahead and moving short distances as fast as she could run. Some of her agility returned with the constant starting and stopping and sprinting. Then the tournament started and she was on her own.

It had been almost two years since her last big tournament at Forest Hills, and there were many people at Wimbledon who felt her injury and her long layoff were handicaps that not even the great Helen Wills could overcome. She played shakily through the early rounds but so superior were her shots and her knowledge of the game that she was able to defeat everyone she played. Then she won the semifinals and found herself in the final round. It was to be a storybook finish. Her opponent in the finals was her bitterest rival, Helen Jacobs.

"I was happy that it was the final match," she has recalled, "because, like the last day of school, it had once seemed so far away."

There was, too, the thrill of playing on the center court at Wimbledon again. It was July 6, 1935, and 19,000 people were jammed into the big stadium. The crowd, which had so often before applauded the marvelous play of the girl in the white eyeshade, now expectantly waited to see if she was anything more than just the shadow of a great player. Miss Jacobs would surely push her to the limit.

Miss Wills' fans took heart as the match got under way. Both girls played steadily, but the superiority of the older was apparent, just as it had usually been in the past. Staying on the baseline where she was forced to do a minimum of running, she kept Miss Jacobs on the run with her accurate shots. She won the set, 6-3.

And then the complexion of the match changed abruptly. Miss Wills, in command only a few moments before, was now on the defensive. She had neither speed nor power and she appeared to be short of breath. Miss Jacobs, gaining confidence, used her backhand with rare skill and won the set, 6-3. It seemed to the crowd that the match was to be a repetition of the one the girls had played two years before at Forest Hills.

Miss Jacobs was still in command as the deciding set got underway. She took the lead, 3-2, then built it to 4-2. Miss Wills, between games, rested wearily on her racquet, then dragged herself back into position. Stepping up the pace, Miss Jacobs won the seventh game with a vicious drive that knocked the racquet from Miss Wills' hand, and now the score stood 5-2.

The eighth game went to deuce and the excitement in the stands rose as the two Helens engaged in long rallies and fierce exchanges. Then Miss Jacobs got an advantage and it was match point. Driving deep into Miss Wills' court, she forced the older girl into a weak return. The ball bounched high for Miss Jacobs and she was set for the kill—a kill she never got. She drove the lob into the net and lost her advantage.

Now Miss Wills had her second wind. "It must have seemed to my friends in the stands that I was going to lose the match," Miss Wills wrote later in her autobiography. "But this did not occupy my thoughts, probably because I had not been in the habit of thinking this way during all the years I played in tournaments. Habits of the past are likely to return to one in critical moments."

Certainly winning was a habit of Helen Wills', and now she thought like a winner. Miss Jacobs' backhand began to falter under the older girl's offensive and the tide of battle changed. Having missed the easy shot which would have given her the set, the match and the championship, Miss Jacobs was never again really in the game. Queen Helen won five games in a row and she was once again the champion of Wimbledon. The crowd stood to accord her an ovation. And Little Miss Poker Face, so calm in every crisis, broke into a big grin and, bubbling over in excitement, rushed off the court and planted a big kiss on the face of the first person she saw. That astonished face belonged to the dignified secretary of the All-England Tennis Club, Sir Herbert Wilberforce.

Helen Wills had a right to be happy. It was her finest moment in tennis.

There are few games that demand as much sustained courage and what Miss Wills liked to call "concentration" as does tennis. The grueling tournaments in the dog days of summer, the marvelous precision in a wide variety of shots that must be maintained despite the intense pressure of a skilled opponent, and the constant planning one must do to set up one's shots all tax the resources of even the most experienced player. Under these conditions it is little wonder that tennis has provided its fans with long afternoons of entertainment even in matches that did not directly involve championships. Two players of exceptional ability, probing each other's flaws and testing each other's courage and endurance, invariably produce a stimulating sight.

Many instances come to mind: there was Bill Talbert, the stylish New Yorker who, though a lifelong diabetic, overcame his handicap to rank with the best players of his time; little Maureen Connolly coming to Forest Hills as a sixteen-year-old bobbysoxer and standing up under the pressure of competing with the most experienced women players in the world; and, perhaps less publicized but unforgettable for anyone who saw it, the remarkable stand that the veteran Frank Parker made against Pancho Gonzales in 1949.

Gonzales was approaching his peak as a player that year. He dominated amateur tennis and, coming up to the National Singles Championship at Forest Hills in August, it was felt that he would have little trouble defending the crown he had won there the previous summer. Standing six feet four inches and powerfully built, this young Californian had one of the most explosive serves in the history of the sport. To it he had added a brilliant all-around game that blasted even far more experienced men off the court. He swept through the early rounds of the tournament and then, in the semifinals came up against Frank Parker. At thirty-three, Parker was twelve years older than the champion. He, too, had held the National Singles title, but that had been during the war when so many of the game's best players were in military service. Since the end of the war he had taken a back seat to the bigger, more powerful men like Jack Kramer, Bob Falkenberg and Gonzales.

And so, on September 4, he took the court against Gonzales. All of the big guns were in the hands of the champion. Parker's only chance to create even the semblance of a contest was to draw on all the guile accumulated through years of tournament competition. Far greater players than Parker, however, had wilted before Gonzales' crushing attack. His guile would have to be augmented by the most determined resistance.

The champion started out as if he were trying to terrorize

Parker before the game got well under way, undermining his resolution and robbing him of his steadiness. Pancho's cannon-ball serve exploded in front of the older man and it seemed a miracle that it did not tear the racquet from his hand. But, after losing the first two points, Parker settled down to combat Gonzales' attack and astonished the crowd by coming back to win the game. Gonzales broke through Parker's service to win the second game but Parker, again performing the rare feat of beating Pancho on the big man's service, went ahead 2-1. Gonzales quickly took the next two games and moved ahead, 3-2. The crowd settled down to watch the slaughter.

It was at this point that Parker began one of the most astonishing exhibitions of the game of tennis that anyone has seen at Forest Hills. Undaunted by Gonzales' fierce attack, Parker seized the initiative and handled Pancho as if he were a novice. Miraculously cool under such pressure, Parker placed each shot perfectly, lobbing the ball high over Gonzales' head, drawing him back in toward the net, and then sending the great champion, looking awkward and confused, racing back toward the baseline again. The rare sound of laughter rose from the stands at Forest Hills as Gonzales floundered under the unexpected turn of events.

"Never before in the experience of this observer," wrote Allison Danzig the next day in the *New York Times*, "has anyone used the lob with such demoralizing precision and not often has anyone combined such baffling, adamantine defensive genius with so much brillance in attacking from every quarter."

It was to Gonzales' credit that he never let up his attack. Trapped in the mesh of Parker's deadly counterattack, frustrated as Parker returned his once invincible service, he fought back bravely. Parker, mixing his shots, volleying crisply and demoralizing Gonzales with his baffling lobs, won four straight games to take the set, 6-3. If Pancho hoped to straighten himself out with the beginning of the second set, he was disappointed.

The applause for Parker's magnificent stand rose now as the veteran moved off in front. Calling on every trick he knew, he frustrated every effort of the champion to get back into the match. When the score mounted to 5-2, Gonzales' situation was desperate. And then the crowd had the opportunity to see a great player fighting with his back to the wall. Pancho's refusal to give in was suddenly rewarded. He fought off disaster at the last possible moment, for it would have been disastrous to trail two sets to none in this best three-out-of-five match. His great serve finally came to his rescue and not even Parker's fighting heart could combat it. Three devastating aces turned the tide in Pancho's favor and he went on to take the second set after some thrilling exchanges, 9-7.

Parker, weakening now, could well have rested on his laurels and submitted quietly. Even at this point, however, he challenged the champion's supremacy. He played with all his old skill but his strength had been drained. While he could set up Gonzales for the shots which had so demoralized him earlier, he no longer was able to execute them. Time after time he rallied but he was only postponing the inevitable now. Gonzales' overwhelming attack had taken its toll. He won the next two sets, 6-3 and 6-2, and the two men walked off the court to the grateful cheers of the crowd. Both men had added another chapter to the story of a sport which has had its share of determined heroes and heroines.

Chapter 8 **Money Pitcher**

One of the most meaningful of all the many expressions in the jargon that baseball has created for itself is "money pitcher." That it is not heard more frequently is an indication that the species of pitcher it celebrates is a rarity, rather than a sign of reluctance on baseball's part to overwork a pet phrase. A money pitcher is one whose lifetime record may not be spectacular but who has the happy knack of being at his best in the games which his team must win to stay in the race. He seldom wins twenty games in a season, he has little success against the second division teams and sometimes he has difficulty in winning more games than he loses. But he is the pitcher that the manager always turns to when his most dangerous rivals are coming to town and he needs a well-pitched game. The money pitcher thrives under pressure which wilts the others. Relishing the taunts of his rivals and the hoots of the crowd, he finds in the fiercest competition the stimulant which rescues him from mediocrity.

Sal Maglie was such a pitcher. He did not reach his prime until he was thirty-three years old, an age when the power has escaped from a pitcher's arm. Alternately crippled by a back injury and drained of his strength by the summer heat, Maglie has left no impressive victory totals by which posterity can measure his skill. But no one who saw him (or hit against him) will ever forget him. Barred for years from the sacred fields of organized baseball because he had defied its rules to pitch in the "outlawed" Mexican League, Maglie brought back to the majors the baffling curve ball and the pinpoint control which were to become the material tools of his success. More than that, his desire to win was seasoned with the meanness he had acquired in years of rough-and-tumble play. The batter who crowded the plate against him was likely to have his skull splintered by what was left of Maglie's fast ball. The grim Italian, his sallow face darkened by the shadow of his heavy beard, his brown eyes hooded by protruding lids, looked, as he glared down on enemy batters, like a Renaissance assassin.

Maglie never fitted the role of a sports "hero." The home crowd admired him, the enemy crowd hated him. His qualities were those of a formidable yet sinister villain. A soft-spoken man who kept to himself around the ball park and spent his time away from there with his family, he had only to walk on the field to arouse the most violent passions. When pitching for the New York Giants he represented, in Brooklyn, everything that was evil. And, becoming a Dodger in one of baseball's most curious cases of transmutation, he threw that excitable borough into confusion. So strong was their antipathy for him that many Brooklyn fans thought it a disgrace that the

Dodgers depended on Maglie to bring them a pennant in 1956. Even the Brooklyn players, whose reflexes had been so conditioned that they nearly foamed at the sight of Maglie, found it hard to erase their traditional feelings about him although he was pitching them to the pennant. Typical of their attitude was the response of Jackie Robinson in a casual conversation with a reporter during the latter part of 1956.

"That Maglie's done a great job for you, Jackie," the reporter said, trying to get a rise out of the Dodgers' star infielder.

"He's a helluva pitcher," Jackie observed, and lapsed back into silence.

"Is he a nice guy?" the reporter asked.

"I don't know anything about that," Robinson said, "but he's a helluva pitcher."

It is a difficult thing to say of a player who, like Maglie, pitched for years up and down the North American continent (and on some of the islands adjacent to it) which achievement was his finest. No one can deny that he was at his peak while pitching for the Giants and that his most typical role was that of smothering the powerful hitters in the Brooklyn lineup. But, ironically, it was in a Brooklyn uniform in 1956 that he acted out his proudest part. Here, against a background of implausible melodrama, he best displayed that combination of courage and skill that had marked his pitching since his return to the big leagues.

"That Maglie is one guy who's got the pitching racket solved," Garry Schumacher, an official of the Giants, once said. Sal, to be sure, didn't solve it overnight. How he came to be the shrewd, remorseless and dramatic pitcher who brought Brooklyn its last pennant is one of the strangest stories baseball has provided.

Because of the special circumstances which kept Maglie for a time out of organized baseball, his early career more nearly resembled those of the journeymen heavyweight fighters, like Archie Moore and Jersey Joe Walcott, than that of a big-league ballplayer. He gave off no bright promise of future glory in the beginning and, during the lean years, he lived a nomadic existence, drifting with the seasons from town to town and setting up shop wherever they were in need of a competent pitcher. There were few who suspected that he would rise above competency. As a boy in Niagara Falls, New York, he was known as a pretty good basketball player. But, right from the beginning, baseball was his sport. He became a professional in 1938 and toiled in the minor leagues until midway in the 1945 season. It is one indication of his mediocrity in the minors that he lost more games than he won, for his record shows 41 victories and 47 defeats. But 1945 was a wartime year and the Giants were as desperate for pitching help as anybody else. The league was made up of players too old or too young. Maglie, deferred in the draft (he had remained out of baseball in 1943 and 1944 to take a job in a defense plant), was one of the few available men whom the Giants thought could give them competent pitching for the remainder of the season. After that the big fellows would be home from the war and Maglie would not be needed. Sal, finishing the season at the Polo Grounds, won five games and lost four, which, considering his minor-league record, was an achievement in itself.

Maglie seemed to be lost in the shuffle in 1946. There were bigger names on the Giant roster now. In Mexico a couple of wealthy promoters were starting their own baseball league, outside the jurisdiction of organized ball in the United States, and they were offering the kind of money which would lure some American stars south of the border. Maglie, receiving an offer, found that the Giants weren't interested in matching it and so left for Mexico. At the time it seemed a move that could not hurt the Giants, who were not counting on him, and one that could only benefit Maglie; not given much of a chance to make good in the majors, he would be able to earn considerable money in Mexico.

Later events made both parties regret the move. When their pitching collapsed in 1946 the Giants plummeted to last place and stayed there. Though they moved out of the cellar in 1947, they were hampered for the next three years by the lack of an outstanding pitcher. Maglie, on his part, was disappointed in the Mexican League, as were most other American players who jumped their contracts to play there. The easy money which had marked the early days of the league soon disappeared. Meanwhile, Maglie had been banned from organized baseball "for life." He could not even pick up extra money on barnstorming tours with other professional players after the season because they were prohibited from playing against an "outlaw." As far as baseball was concerned, Maglie *was* an outlaw.

In the winters Maglie pitched in the Caribbean islands, then migrated to Canada to join semipro teams there in the summers. And it was in these out-of-the-way places that he refined the skills that enabled him to seize his big chance when it came his way. Pitching in all kinds of weather, on all kinds of fields and against players of varying talent, he became immune to the little incidents which can upset many of the big leagues' pampered and temperamental stars. He also came to know what a dog-eat-dog game baseball really is. When he came back to the Giants he had acquired the hardness that made his name notorious in the National League. Baseball is a man's game, and Maglie played it that way.

It was 1950 when he came back. The commissioner of baseball, alarmed by threats of some of the "outlaws" to sue the game because it was depriving them of their jobs, commuted their life sentences and they flocked back to their original teams. Almost all of them had lost, somewhere along the way, the fine edge which had once established them as big-league players. Of them all, only Maglie had improved. While he did not have overpowering speed, he had perfected a curve ball which made the finest hitters look awkward as they poked at it.

"Maglie's curve is just different from anybody else's," Roy Campanella once said. "I've caught a lot of curve balls and hit a lot of them, but let me tell you, buddy, Maglie's is positively the best!"

This was the time when the Brooklyn team, which had been put together by Branch Rickey, was finally reaching its peak. The Dodgers were the bullyboys of the National League. Their lineup was starred with an array of right-handed sluggers probably unequaled in the league's history. They were especially tough in Ebbets Field, where the inviting walls seemed to rise just at a pitcher's back and where the howling mobs could jar the nerves even of experienced players. It was in this setting that Maglie was at his best. He infuriated both Brooklyn's players and their fans. Knowing every batter's weakness, he pitched accordingly, first throwing a ball under the hitter's chin to drive him back from the plate, then coming

Joe DiMaggio crosses the plate with the first of his two homers against Boston on June 29. Sparked by "The Clipper's" great comeback, the Yankees went on to win the game and the important series.

*Clint Frank of Yale carries the ball against Harvard
in the final game of a great career.*

*Jim Braddock crosses a left to Max Baer
in the first round of his thrilling
comeback from oblivion to win
the 1935 Heavyweight Championship.*

Walter Johnson, "The Big Train," pitching in the 1924 World Series, gets his last chance to perform in the diamond classic. Johnson's lifetime record has never been equaled.

*Glenn Cunningham crosses
the finish line to set a
world's record of 4:06.7
for the mile at the Princeton
Invitation Meet in 1934,
beating Bonthron and Venzke,
his most persistent rivals.*

1

2

(UPI)
(UPI)

*Four moments in the historic race when
Roger Bannister broke the barrier
of the four-minute mile. Bannister,
fourth from the right at the start (1),
trails Chris Brasher (2)
and then Chris Chataway (3)
before his final spurt to the tape
(4) as jubilant fans
and officials look on.*

3

4

Helen Jacobs (left) and Helen Wills walking
onto the court at Wimbledon for their thrilling
final match in 1935. The latter won
after being one point from defeat.

(UPI)

*Sal Maglie pitching
against the Phillies
finally wins his
first no-hitter
in the twilight
of his diamond life.*

(UPI)

*Fighting fatigue and
pain, Ben Hogan
manages a smile after
tying for first place in
the 1950 National Open
at the Merion Golf Club.
Hogan went on to win
the playoff
the following day.*

Doak Walker, the little man in pro football,
plows through the New York Yankee line
for a Detroit Lion touchdown.

Tony Zale (left) takes a hard right from Rocky Graziano in the third round of their rematch in 1947. Zale lost the middleweight title on a TKO in the sixth round, but regained it in their third meeting.

Count Turf, with Conn McCreary up, driving for the finish to win the seventy-seventh running of the Kentucky Derby in 1951.

*With nothing left but his heart
and his "nothing ball," Dizzy Dean held the Yankees
for seven innings in the second game
of the 1938 World Series.*

Campanella scores against Pittsburgh in a jarring play at home as Pirate catcher Sandlock loses the ball.

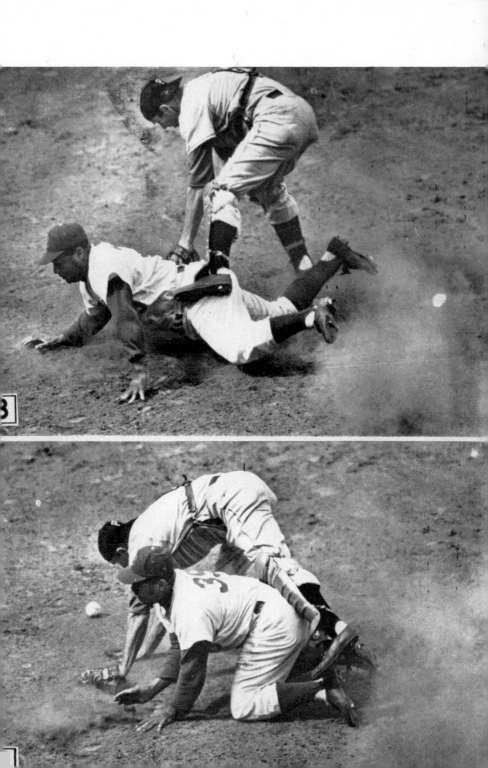

Bobby Thomson brings a climax to "the little miracle of Coogan's Bluff" as he nears home plate and his jubilant teammates after hitting the historic home run that beat the Dodgers in the final playoff game for the 1951 National League pennant.

*Kyle Rote carries around end against Notre Dame
in the thrilling game in which the Mustangs of SMU
nearly upset the favored Fighting Irish.*

*The scoreboard tells
the dramatic story of the final
moments in Don Larsen's
unprecedented perfect
World Series game.
This pitch struck out
the last Dodger batter,
Dale Mitchell,
as second baseman Billy Martin
waits tensely.*

Torger Tokle goes into his "power dive" as he hurdles
the mountain tops on this jump of 263 feet
in the 1942 Seattle Ski Club open jumping tournament.

back with that tantalizing curve ball over the outside corner. The hitter, pushed back on his heels by the previous pitch, could only lunge awkwardly at the curve. Occasionally a hitter would not be able to get out of the way of the brush-back pitch in time and it would hit him.

"Beanballs!" cried the hitters, and the madder they got the more tense they were as they approached the plate, and Maglie's job became that much easier.

"Spitballs!" the hitters cried when that curve ball dipped away from them and they beat it weakly into the dirt. As they had never seen a curve ball like Maglie's, they felt that it must be guided either by magic or a foreign substance. Looking at "Sinister Sal," as they called him, standing there on the mound, they could not be quite sure, but it was easier to complain about spitballs. Maglie, unperturbed by their complaints and the sometimes vicious insults of the crowd, became the leader of the resistance which kept the Dodgers from completely dominating the league. He made the Giants serious contenders in 1950 by winning eighteen games (he lost only four), then played the biggest role in the remarkable surge which overtook the Dodgers in the course of 1951's "Miracle Pennant." His record was 23-6 that season, the most impressive he ever had.

It was at this time that his chronic back trouble became more conspicuous. Through the next three and a half seasons with the Giants he was often unable to pitch and there were times when it appeared that his career was at end. But the day would always arrive when the Giants were faced with an important ball game, usually against the Dodgers, and Leo Durocher would turn to his money pitcher. Sal would go to the mound, pitch with all of the considerable wile and courage at his command, and he would again be the unbeatable pitcher of old. At times his competitive urge seemed to border on the venomous, and other competitive players like Jackie Robinson would seek revenge by dropping bunts along the first base-line, hoping to draw Maglie over to make a play, and then run him down. Sal was bumped and bruised a few times, but these tactics had no effect on his system of pitching. The next time a batter crowded the plate against him you could be sure that a fast ball would be aimed in the direction of his head.

"When I'm pitching I figure that plate is mine," Maglie said, "and I don't like anybody getting too close to it."

Maglie's eighteen victories kept the Giants in the 1952 pennant race until the last week of the season, when the Dodgers moved off by themselves to win. Nineteen fifty-three was a frustrating year for him. Crippled by back trouble, he sat idly on the bench through most of the season and watched the Dodgers run away with the flag. He won only eight games but, on the few occasions he was able to pitch against the Dodgers, he was as tough for them as he had ever been. And then it was 1954 and he and the Giants wiped out the bitter memories of the previous year. Sal won fourteen games, including four victories over the Dodgers, and the Giants went on to win the pennant and the World Series.

As the 1955 season opened, Maglie had every reason to be optimistic. The Giants were the defending world champions; Sal was still as baffling to enemy hitters as before; and he retained the mastery over the Dodgers, baseball's most powerful group of sluggers, that had enabled him to beat them 22 times in 30 decisions since he had come into the league. He started the season well, but by the end of July his record was 9-5 and his recent performances had not been encouraging.

"I guess you could say that 'rest' is my biggest problem," Sal said to a reporter at that time. "In the spring, when it was cool and I could have used the work to sharpen my control, I was getting too much rest between starts. But now, when it's hot as hell and my back is giving me some trouble, a couple of our other pitchers are hurt and I've been starting two and three times a week."

There was no longer a race in the National League. The Dodgers, with a spectacular early spurt, had moved so far out in front that no one had a chance to catch them. The seven other teams were now preparing for the future, and the Giants did not see Maglie in theirs. Their attendance had fallen off as interest in the race waned and they were looking for ways to cut expenses. The $35,000 salary they were paying a pitcher who was thirty-eight years old and whose lame back might end his career at any moment seemed a luxury they could not afford. There might still be a few victories left in Maglie's right arm, but they would not affect the outcome of the pennant race. Better to clear away the dead wood and make room for the younger pitchers who needed the experience. As the other National League clubs felt the same way about him, the Giants went looking for a buyer in the American League. The Yankees, battling Cleveland for the pennant there, needed pitching help and were willing to take a chance on the aging money pitcher. Cleveland, whose strength lay in its pitching, also put in a bid for Maglie, solely as a means of keeping him out of the hands of the Yankees.

It was July 31 and the Dodgers had moved a step closer to the pennant by beating the Cardinals in St. Louis. They were talking idly among themselves in the bus outside the ball park, waiting to be driven back to their hotel. Then a club official climbed into the bus, sat down next to one of the players and said, "The Giants just sold Maglie to the Indians. I heard it on the radio."

It wasn't said in a loud voice, but somehow every player in the bus picked it up. "The Giants sold Maglie!" This was no mere scrap of trade gossip. To others it might have meant only the sale of a broken-down pitcher to a club in the other league. But it was big news to the Dodgers.

After a moment Don Hoak, who was then playing third base and leading off for the Dodgers, shouted, "Well, at least we won't have to face that slob again."

"Oh, yeah?" came a voice from the back of the bus. "You'll be leading off against him in the first game of the World Series."

That remark was a measure of the respect in which the Dodgers held their old foe. They believed that, with Maglie on their side, the Indians would beat out the Yankees for the pennant. Then, despite the wealth of fine pitchers on their staff, Sal would be the Indians' natural choice to open the World Series against Brooklyn. Through the Dodgers' bravado was clearly seen the relief which they felt at his passing from the National League, and also the uneasiness with which they contemplated facing him in the Series.

But Maglie was not to be a miracle man in 1955. His back still bothered him in Cleveland and he was unimpressive in the few starts he made there. The Indians, having achieved their purpose in keeping him away from the Yankees, relied chiefly on their other pitchers. It did them no good. The Yankees went on to win the pennant. With no Maglie to mar their sense of well being, the Dodgers beat the Yankees in the Series and brought Brooklyn its first world championship.

When Maglie returned to his home in Niagara Falls that winter it seemed that his career was sputtering to an inglorious close. His pride had been hurt not only by the brusqueness with which the Giants had discarded him, but by the knowledge that no other team in the National League had been willing to gamble on him. He felt that Cleveland, with its rich pitching staff, had little use for him. Because they would understandably give their younger pitchers most of the assignments during spring training, Sal would have little chance to get the work that he needed to sharpen his own pitching tools.

"During the winter I got a letter from Hank Greenberg, the Indians' general manager," Maglie has recalled, "and he said he was sorry but he'd have to cut my salary because, in reality, I would be starting all over again in the spring, trying to win a job with the club. He told me that they would look me over carefully and give me every chance to make it. But from the tone of his letter it didn't look as if I'd even make it to their training camp."

If Greenberg had been able to find a buyer for Maglie's contract, Sal wouldn't have made it to the Indians' camp. Greenberg went to most of the other teams, trying to get them to take Sal off his hands, so that he could get a return on his original investment. But there were no takers, not even among the weaker teams who desperately needed pitchers. Sal was considered a has-been. He reported to the Indians' camp several days ahead of the other players and worked harder than the most ambitious rookie. He was so determined to make the best of the slight chance he had that he gave up smoking in the hope of increasing his stamina.

"I may be thirty-nine years old," he said to a friend, "but I have a young arm. I'm a long way from being finished."

There were few who shared his optimism. His chances to pitch for Cleveland were not frequent enough to keep him in shape, and so he did not look impressive when he did pitch. When the season began he made only two brief appearances in relief for the Indians. It was in the unlikely environs of Jersey City that Sal got his reprieve from oblivion. The Dodgers, who had made an agreement to play seven of their games that year in Jersey City's Roosevelt Stadium, also threw in an exhibition game in an effort to get back some of the money they had poured out to reclaim the ball park. Cleveland agreed to be their opponents. Starting their first eastern swing of the season, the Indians did not want to waste any of their best pitchers in such a game. One of those chosen to pitch against the Dodgers, therefore, was Maglie.

Sal pitched four innings and the Dodgers were amazed to find that the pitcher they had left for dead a year before had somehow come back from the grave. One by one the doubting Thomases in the Brooklyn lineup went up to the plate, swung incredulously at the Maglie curve ball and found it was the same pitch that had felled them in the past. They could get only one harmless single against him. Evidently somebody had forgotten to drive the stake through Maglie's remorseless heart.

Now it was the middle of May and the Indians had to cut down their roster to the player limit. Maglie's days in Cleveland were numbered. Among the general managers Greenberg called was Buzzie Bavasi of the Dodgers. "He can still help a ball club, Buzzie, I'm sure of that," Greenberg said. "But with all the young pitchers we have, there just isn't room for him here. You can have him for the asking."

The Dodgers needed pitching help. The staff that had helped them to the world championship the year before was floundering. Bavasi told Greenberg he would call him back, then went into action. First he called Walt Alston, the Dodgers' manager.

"We've got a chance to pick up Maglie," Bavasi told him. "What do you think?"

"He looked mighty good to me in Jersey City," Alston said. "I'd say grab him. I think he can help us."

Bavasi then put in a call to the Dodgers' veteran captain and shortstop, Pee Wee Reese. "Pee Wee, you hit against Maglie when he was with the Giants and you hit against him the other night in Jersey City. What do you think of him now?"

"Why?" Pee Wee asked.

"We have a chance to get him."

"Buzzie, I honestly couldn't see any difference. He looked like the same guy to me."

"Do you think we should take a gamble and get him?"

"I'd like to see him on our side," the Dodger captain said.

Bavasi needed the approval of one man—Walter O'Malley, the owner of the Dodgers. O'Malley, who has the enterprising spirit of an old-time fight manager and will grasp at anything that has a new "twist" to it, whether it is a minor promotion stunt to lure a few customers to the ball park on a dull evening or a plan to upset the map of baseball, liked the idea of seeing the old Dodger killer in a Dodger uniform. It made little difference if he won any games in Brooklyn; the irony of the move would draw fans to the ball park.

And so Sal Maglie, in one of the most startling of all baseball deals, became a Dodger. The Indians sold him to Brooklyn for only $1,000, which also made the deal one of baseball's biggest bargains. Joining the team, Sal occupied a unique position at Ebbets Field. The Brooklyn players, though they found it difficult to warm up to him, were obviously pleased to have him on their side. They no longer shouted "Beanball!" when one of his close pitches drove a batter back from the plate; they only marveled at his skill in setting up the batter for his best pitch. They no longer complained bitterly that he resorted to a spitter when in trouble; they praised the curve ball which was "different" from any they had ever seen.

And now the breaks began to come Maglie's way. He was with a team which needed his help. He was pitching at Ebbets Field, the park where he had always enjoyed his most spectacular success. And the heat which had drained his strength the previous summer did not settle on New York during the dog days of July and August in 1956. Maglie impressed Alston in a couple of tune-up performances, then stepped into the breach when the Dodgers needed him most. Beginning a western trip in Chicago, the Dodgers were jolted by the loss of three straight games to the Cubs. From Chicago the Dodgers traveled to Milwaukee and Alston feared that another such disastrous series would knock his team out of the race. The Braves were their most threatening rivals. Maglie came to Alston on the day that the series opened.

"Would I help you out if I pitched tonight?" he asked.

"Hell, yes," Alston, who had planned to use Sal later in the week, said.

"Well, I think I'm ready to go nine innings," Maglie said. He was. He walked out to the mound before a screaming pro-Milwaukee crowd at County Stadium (how often he had pitched brilliantly in front of similarly hostile crowds in Ebbets Field!) and shut out the Braves with three hits. During the succeeding six weeks Maglie made nine more starts for the Dodgers. He won two of them and lost three, but in most of those games the team did not hit behind him and he usually had to be taken out for a pinch hitter. In the three games he lost over that stretch of time the Dodgers scored a total of only four runs. Alston saved him for the toughest jobs, and eight of his first fifteen starts were made against the Dodgers' two leading contenders, the Braves and the Reds.

It is easy to pin point both the date and the cause of the change in Sal's fortunes. The date was July 28 and the cause, as improbable as it sounds, stemmed from the thirty-nine-year-old Maglie's entrance into Brooklyn's regular pitching rotation, working every fourth day.

"From the time the Giants sold me in July, '55, until I started working regularly with the Dodgers," Maglie explained, "I was pretty much on vacation. Did it help me? Let's say this—it sure didn't hurt me. I came back stronger than I'd been in years. Rest, of course, strengthened my arm and my back, but I've found when my arm gets strong it gets tight, too, and then I don't have good control. Only regular work improves my control and regular work means pitching with only three or four days' rest. I can still pitch that often when the weather isn't too hot."

This was the most incredible part of Maglie's comeback—that the veteran was able to win not only the *big* games for the Dodgers, but that he had the stamina to go out and win the little ones in between. From July 28 until the end of the season he won ten games and lost only two and had an earned run average of 1.88. The two games he lost were by scores of 2-1 and 3-2. Twelve times during the season's last two months he pitched with only three days' rest.

Maglie pitched one of his most important games of the year against the Braves on September 11. It was the opener

of a two-game series, the last of the year between the two
contenders, and Milwaukee came into Ebbets Field leading
the Dodgers by one game. Maglie was matched with Bob
Buhl, who had beaten the Dodgers seven straight times. It
was a game that demanded heroics, that demanded a money
pitcher. At the end of seven innings the Dodgers were leading,
2-1. Eddie Mathews had brought in the only run off Maglie,
hitting a home run in the second inning. The Dodgers got
their runs in the fourth when an old man named Maglie came
to bat with the bases filled and drove in two runs with a
single. Then the Braves got the potential tying run to third
base in the eighth inning. There were two men out, but the
powerful Mathews was coming to bat. Sal was obviously tired
and Alston had two relief pitchers ready in the bullpen. The
manager walked out to the mound to talk to his pitcher.

"What do you want to do?" Alston asked.

"I got to pitch to this guy," Maglie said.

Alston turned around and went back to the dugout. Maglie
pitched to Mathews and got him. The Dodgers won the game.
Then later that week, when the Reds, who had been making
threatening noises, invaded Ebbets Field, Maglie again got
the assignment in the opening game of the series and throttled
Cincinnati's big hitters to win, 3-2.

But, for all of Maglie's marvelous pitching, the Dodgers
could not get a grip on first place. When they dug in at
Ebbets Field for the last week of the season they were wobbling badly and once more trailed the Braves by a full game.
This time the Phillies were their opponents. Alston, in desperation, turned to Maglie, banking on him to stave off a complete
collapse. Seldom has a pitcher risen to a critical situation in
the manner that Maglie did on that late September evening. He

pitched the first no-hit, no-run game of his long career. Each
inning the din grew louder as the fans, once fervent and dedi-
cated enemies of this tough, unrelenting competitor, now
prayed for him and cheered and shouted encouragement. He
walked grimly to the mound in the ninth inning, protecting
both a 5-0 lead and his no-hitter, and retired the first two
Philadelphia batters. He hit the next batter, Richie Ashburn,
with a pitch, and then worked on Marv Blaylock. Blaylock hit
a ground ball to the Brooklyn second baseman, Junior Gilliam.

"I watched the ball bounce all the way," Maglie said afterward. "I watched every damn hop until Gilliam got it and
Hodges grabbed his throw and the ump's arm went up for
the out."

The Dodgers, on the wings of this tremendous psychological lift, pressed the Braves now, and it was the Milwaukee
team which faltered. Playing Pittsburgh in a doubleheader on
September 28, the Dodgers had a chance to move into first
place by winning both games. Maglie, who had gained his no-
hitter only four nights before, pitched the first game. Again he
was magnificent. He gave up a two-run home run in the first
inning, then held the Pirates to two singles over the last eight
innings and the Dodgers won, 6-2. They also won the second
and moved permanently into first place. The season ended the
next day.

Sal had finished the season with a record of 13-5 and an
earned run average of 2.92. The pitcher on whom nobody
had wanted to gamble had come back to win the season's
most important games for the Dodgers. And, when not playing, he had given the team's younger pitchers the valuable
advice which enabled them to contribute to Brooklyn's triumph. There was no finer tribute to Maglie's importance to

the Dodgers than Jackie Robinson's comment:

"He molded our pitching staff," Robinson said of his old
foe, "and then he educated it."

There is a postscript to the story. Now that the Dodgers
were unexpectedly in the World Series there was no doubt
that Maglie would pitch the first game against the Yankees. He
had pitched a no-hitter and he wanted to add a Series triumph
to his list of achievements before time ran out on him. He had
failed to win a game against the Yankees in 1951 and, though
pitching exceptionally during the Giants' rout of the Indians in
1954, he had not received credit for the game he worked; he
had been taken out before Dusty Rhodes hit the winning home
run. But now he pitched against the mighty Yankees and they
proved no more of a problem for him in that first game than
had the opposing National League teams during the season.
He survived early home runs by Mickey Mantle and Billy
Martin to hold the Yankees scoreless after the fourth inning,
piling up an exceptional total of ten strike-outs and winning,
6-3. After the game, Hank Bauer, one of the Yankees' fiercest
competitors, remarked, "Maglie fights you on every pitch."

The most memorable game of the Series was the fifth. It was
probably the most important, too, because in winning it the
Yankees cleared the way for their eventual victory that year.
Maglie's opponent was Don Larsen. No batter reached base
against either pitcher until the fourth inning when Mantle
hit a home run against Maglie. Sal then escaped further trouble
when Duke Snider made a tumbling catch of Yogi Berra's
sinking line drive. But that one run was enough to send Maglie
to defeat, for Larsen went on to pitch the first perfect game
in World Series history, retiring all twenty-seven batters he
faced. However, it was Maglie who lifted Larsen's perform-

ance out of the category of an ornament and made it almost a necessity. He battled Larsen to the finish.

After Mantle's home run it appeared that Maglie's great arm had at last run down. Almost everything he threw for the next two innings was a line drive and only the alert Dodger defense kept the Yankees from getting more than the one additional run they scored in the sixth. The second-guessers in the stands were beginning to shake their heads and mournfully intone that Alston was making a mistake. Maglie was through and he should be taken out.

But they were still underestimating the competitive flame within the old pitcher. He refused to believe the signs that told him he had nothing left. He seemed to catch his second wind in the seventh inning and he breezed by the Yankees. Then he went to the mound in the eighth inning, the last he was to pitch that year, and struck out the side.

The Dodgers lost the game, 2-0. Larsen that day was invincible. But the incredible Maglie, the money pitcher, was as heroic in defeat as he had been all year in victory.

Chapter 9   Doak the Giant Killer

Doak Walker's professional football debut in Detroit had aroused curiosity rather than excitement there. The size of his college reputation seemed offset by his own physical size—less than adequate when compared to that of the brawny old pros around him. The Detroit Lions had opened on the road, easily beating Green Bay. While Doak had played his part by kicking two field goals, there was nothing to suggest he had established himself in football's big league. And, if ordinarily there would have been a lot of publicity for the rookie halfback, it was submerged under the deluge of baseball news as the Tigers dueled the Yankees for the pennant. The Lions could not even open their home season at familiar Briggs Stadium. As the Tigers were still playing baseball there, the Lions took over the smaller field at the University of Detroit.

It was September 24, 1950. Nineteen thousand fans gathered

under a dreary sky to watch the Lions play the Pittsburgh
Steelers, a rugged defensive team which had beaten Detroit
in an exhibition game only a few weeks before. "I wasn't especially confident, but I wasn't scared," Doak was to say
later. "Let's just say I was hopeful."

The crowd sent up a cheer when Walker's name was announced; it was hopeful, too. As soon as the game started the
crowd began to lose some of its optimism. The Steelers threw
up an unyielding defense. Both teams played warily, looking
for a break. This in itself was unusual in the wide-open pro
league. There was only one break in the pattern during the
first half, and it provided the half's most thrilling moment. On
fourth down, with 27 yards to go for a first down, Walker
went back to punt. But, when the pass from center was poor
and the aggressive Pittsburgh line bore down on him, he decided not to kick. Tucking the ball under his arm, he eluded
two linemen and raced around right end. Picking up his
blockers and feinting several other tacklers out of position,
Doak gained 29 yards and the vital first down which carried
the Lions out of trouble.

Neither team scored in that half. As the second half opened,
however, the Steelers took the ball and marched 72 yards for a
touchdown. Trailing 7-0 now, the Lions fought back. Late in
the third period quarterback Bobby Layne began to hit his
pass receivers for long gains. As the period ended the Lions
moved to a first down on Pittsburgh's 11-yard line. In the
huddle Layne called for another pass—this time to Walker.
When the ball was put in play, Doak sprinted to his left
and, closely guarded by Pittsburgh's fine defensive back, Lynn
Chandnois, headed for the end zone. Layne's pass was there
when Doak turned around. He and Chandnois went up for

the ball and it was Doak who came down with it.

Now the score was 7-6, and Walker got set to try for the extra point. Then, just as the teams lined up, the Lions' coaches on the sidelines realized they had only ten men on the field. An eleventh man was hurriedly dispatched. As the ball was snapped to Layne, who was holding for the try from placement, the new man rushed into position. Doak, unruffled, kicked the ball between the uprights and it was a tie game.

Both teams pulled out all stops now, but the score remained 7-7 into the closing minutes of the game. Then, with the ball deep in Detroit territory, Walker was forced to punt. He got the ball off beautifully, long and high, giving the Lions' tacklers a chance to race downfield under it. When Pittsburgh's safety man, Bobby Gage, caught it he was hit hard and he fumbled. The Lions recovered on the Steelers' 15.

The crowd came alive now. There were less than three minutes to play. Here the Steelers' defense, so formidable all afternoon, stiffened again and three running plays failed. It was fourth down and, with time running out, the Lions would not get another chance to score. Layne called for a field goal. With Bobby holding the ball on the 20-yard line, Walker kicked and it was good. A few moments later the game ended and Detroit had its victory, 10-7.

There was no doubt who had been the hero in that rugged game. Walker, gaining 87 yards in 16 rushes at the big Pittsburgh line, punting well and scoring all of the Lions' points, had played remarkably. "But," as somebody said later, "he looks so small."

This was the rap against Doak Walker when he left college to meet the challenge of the National Football League. A man standing five feet, eleven inches, weighing almost 170 pounds and built along the rugged lines of Walker is considered a marvelous physical specimen in most fields of life. Complement Doak's body with one of the most memorable careers in the history of college football and you are tempted to say that he could be a star wherever he played. But the pros did not jump to that conclusion. Such is the essence of professional football that Walker was viewed with as little awe as David commanded when he set out to challenge Goliath. And remember that the rules did not permit Doak to carry a slingshot.

The pros' opinions of Walker's chances were founded on experience. Size and power mean more in the NFL than a barrel of All-America citations, and many college hot shots have strutted into the pro league only to find that the pace was much too punishing for them. Walker, though his astonishing accomplishments in college placed him on a level well above even the usual All-America player, seemed handicapped in other ways. His weight of 170 pounds, considered the absolute minimum for success in the NFL (except at quarterback in the T formation, where the special nature of the job usually relieves the player of the more arduous running and blocking assignments), tended to dip well below that as the season progressed. In his junior year at Southern Methodist University Doak dropped to 163 pounds. At the same time his years as a high school and college football hero, during which he was the major objective of every opposing team's defense, seemed to have taken their toll of his body. Where before he had always been his team's "iron man," Doak was frequently on the bench during his final year in college, and missed three games completely because of injury and illness. The constant mauling he could expect to get at the hands of 265-pound tackles in the pro league was not designed to return anyone to a state of health and happiness.

Eddie Anderson, who coached the College All-Star squad of which Walker was a member just after his graduation from SMU, probably shared the feelings of many of Doak's admirers. Having watched the little halfback run through a number of practice sessions (Doak was never at his best in practice), Anderson began to suspect that the nasty old pros might devour him at a gulp. One afternoon he took him aside and said, "Doak, you're too nice for the pros. If I were you I'd go home."

Anderson, like so many other football men, underestimated this young player who had instinctively risen to meet every crisis during his glamorous undergraduate days at SMU. Doak was the ideal All-American—Frank Merriwell and Jack Armstrong come to life. He was handsome; he was endowed with the ability to maintain his poise, yet never lose his competitive fire, under the most remorseless pressure; he was devoted to clean living and fair play; he was the most talented all-around college player of his time; and through it all he remained a model of boyish modesty, even refusing to read the accounts of his triumphs in the newspapers. Plaster saints have an alarming tendency to come apart when they fall in among the beer-drinking, eye-gouging troglodytes who infest professional football. Walker was to demonstrate that the thorny path of virtue can lead to a hardness all its own.

He was carefully groomed for his role. His father, Ewell Doak Walker, Sr., had been an enthusiastic but undistinguished football player at Austin College in Sherman, Texas. He became a teacher and, later, a school administrator, but his enthusiasm for football did not diminish. When little Doak came along, on New Year's Day, 1927, the elder Walker decided that he would raise him to be a football player. He did not limit his son's education to the football field, however. He was fortunately aware of the absurdity of developing a boy's body to the complete neglect of his mind and character.

Doak learned his lessons well. At the age of two he was having regulation footballs tossed at him by his father. At the age of six he was place-kicking over the clothesline in the Walker's back yard. His father schooled him in all of the fundamentals of the sport and gave him valuable advice on how to keep his body relaxed and supple in the midst of furious action. During the summers Doak was packed off to camp, where he played a variety of sports and toughened his already sturdy little body. At home he was in bed at eight o'clock every night, a habit which became so instilled in him that even in college he seldom stayed up beyond ten o'clock. Yet his father also tried to give him a sense of proportion. "Remember, Doak," he told him, "football is only a game. When it gets to the point where it isn't fun any more, that's the time to quit."

That Doak was not growing as big as his father might have hoped did not keep him from standing out among his schoolmates. His natural ability, sharpened by long hours of practice with his father, earned him a great deal of attention around Dallas. When he entered Highland Park High School there, he was an all-around star, and gathered more letters and captaincies than any other player in the school's history. With him in the backfield and a year ahead of him in school was Bobby Layne, a boy who was also to leave his mark on Southwestern football.

The careers of these two young Dallas players became curiously intertwined. Layne, after his graduation from Highland Park, went to the University of Texas and performed brilliantly there as a freshman. Then, when Doak had finished high school, they both entered the Merchant Marine. Layne tried to talk his friend into enrolling at Texas after their service with the Merchant Marine had ended, but a meeting with Layne's head coach, Blair Cherry, never developed and Doak finally settled on SMU. He had grown up near the SMU campus, had idolized the SMU players as a boy, and now his old head coach at Highland Park, Rusty Russell, had joined the SMU staff as its backfield coach.

The 1945 football season was half over when Doak joined the SMU squad. The Mustangs had lost four of their six games, and their followers held out little hope that they would improve. But suddenly, sparked by their freshman halfback, they came to life. Meeting a powerful Texas squad they put up a splendid battle. In the first half Walker raced thirty-seven yards for a touchdown, putting the Mustangs ahead, 7-0. In the second half, Doak's pal, Layne, threw two touchdown passes to pull out the game for Texas, 12-7. Walker and Layne walked off the field arm in arm, and went out on a double date.

SMU had lost to Texas, but they were rapidly improving as the season closed and everybody in the state knew all about Doak Walker. Despite his limited service he was selected for the all-Southwest Conference team, and he played in the East-West Game at San Francisco on New Year's Day. He was one of the few freshmen ever to play in this game, but he gave a demonstration of the poise and audacity that were to characterize his play later on. Walker was sent in at halfback in the last quarter when the West was trailing, 7-0. As he did not like the way the quarterback was calling the plays, Doak went into the huddle and said, "The coach told me to take over."

Babe Hollingberry, who was coaching the West squad that day, was startled a moment later to see Walker throw a forward pass. He was especially startled because he had sent orders to the quarterback to concentrate on running, rather than passing. When Doak threw a couple of more passes, Hollingberry turned to a player who had just left the game and asked, "Who's calling the plays in there?"

"Why, Walker is, Coach," he said. "He told us that you sent him in to take over."

"The hell I did!" Hollingberry roared. Then, as he watched Walker guide his team toward the enemy's goal, Babe's face softened. "Well, he's getting results. Let's see what happens."

Walker, running and passing, led the West to a touchdown and the game ended in a tie, 7-7.

Doak spent the 1946 season in the Army but, with his return, SMU embarked on one of the brightest eras in its athletic history. While the Mustangs did not have an impressive all-around team, their little halfback engineered triumphs over the finest clubs in the West. Santa Clara, Missouri, Oklahoma A&M, Rice and UCLA fell before the "The Doaker" and his teammates. Texas loomed next on SMU's schedule, and they were formidable opponents, having averaged four touchdowns a game as they ground out six straight victories. Layne had an outstanding day for Texas, spearheading two touchdown drives, but Walker, scoring SMUs final touchdown and kicking the decisive extra points, was the finest player on the field. Southern Methodist won, 14-13.

Walker, running, passing, punting, place-kicking, blocking, tackling and calling the plays, carried SMU undefeated and untied into the final game of the season. Texas Christian was the last obstacle. It was a magnificent game, crammed with the thrills which are the spice of a traditional contest, and SMU was on the verge of winning with less than a minute to play. Then Texas Christian, with a desperate effort, scored a touchdown in two quick plays and went ahead, 19-13. It was a stunning blow to SMU. As the two teams took their positions for the ensuing kickoff, one of the Texas Christian players passed Walker and grinned.

"What are you going to do now, Doak?" he asked.

Walker stared back at him. "We're going to score," he said.

Texas Christian kicked off and Walker, grabbing the ball, feinted beautifully and then set out in the opposite direction. He raced along the sidelines past clutching defenders. As he darted by the SMU bench he shouted, "Send in Johnson." Then, after running 56 yards, he was finally tackled on Texas Christian's 34 yard line. Gil Johnson, SMU's experienced forward passer, rushed into the game. On the next play Johnson heaved a long pass to the 9 yard line, where Walker made an incredible catch. With time running out, Doak set off for a corner of the end zone on the next play, and was immediately surrounded by Texas Christian defenders. Johnson calmly lobbed a pass to Sid Halliday, unnoticed in the other corner, and the game ended in a tie, 19-19.

That Walker had missed the extra point which would have broken the tie did not matter to his admirers. His performance that day was already one of the finest in Southwest Conference history. He had completed 10 of his 14 passes, he had averaged 54 yards on three kickoff returns, he had thrilled the crowd with runs of 80, 61 and 56 yards, and he had scored SMU's first two touchdowns.

SMU, invited to the Cotton Bowl on New Year's Day, tied a powerful Penn State team, 13-13. Doak scored one of his team's touchdowns, passed for the other. At the season's end he was given the Maxwell Club Award in Philadelphia as the finest college player of 1947, the first time it had been won by a sophomore. Speaking at the award dinner, Bert Bell, the commissioner of professional football, said of Doak:

"Never in my time, and that covers quite a period, have I known a football player that could do so many things so well. He gained a reputation as an offensive player but the records show that he is even better defensively."

Walker played through another brilliant season in 1948. Bobby Layne had graduated from Texas and was playing pro ball with the Detroit Lions, but this did not diminish Doak's incentive. He scored twice, once on a 67-yard run, passed for a third touchdown and kicked all three extra points as SMU beat Texas, 21-6. He injured his leg before the Texas A&M game, and there was doubt that he would play. Coach Matty Bell, realizing that the Aggies would hit the injured leg every chance they got, told Doak to bandage *both* legs. He hoped that this would sufficiently confuse the Aggies to make them forget which leg Doak had injured. The great little halfback, playing in intense pain, accounted for all three of the Mustangs' touchdowns and SMU won, 20-14. But perhaps Doak endeared himself to his fans most in SMU's game against Missouri. It was a losing cause. Missouri proved too powerful for the Mustangs that day and those who saw the game said later that they would have won by five touchdowns had not Walker played so valiantly in defeat. He made a number of breathtaking catches of forward passes, scored one touchdown and set up another, intercepted two Missouri passes at the SMU goal line and caught two runners in the open field.

SMU's Southwestern Conference record was marred only by another tie with Texas Christian. Invited to the Cotton Bowl again on New Year's Day, the Mustangs beat the University of Oregon, 21-12. Doak completed six of his ten passes, quick-kicked 80 yards and blocked ferociously for teammate Kyle Rote, who did most of the running. After SMU's last touchdown, Doak went to the bench and asked Coach Bell if tackle Joe Ethridge could kick the extra point. Ethridge had practiced his place-kicking diligently all season, preparing for an emergency in which Walker might be unable to play. Now, in the last game, Ethridge had taken a ribbing from his teammates as the kicker who had never kicked. Bell gave his permission, Ethridge kicked and his aim was true. It was one of the many gracious gestures for which Doak was admired.

He was on everybody's All-America team that year (he had also made the Associated Press All-America as a sophomore) and he was named the country's outstanding player by the Heisman Committee and by *Sport Magazine*. But it had been a punishing season for him. His weight had dropped to 163 pounds, he had been injured in several games and, as his fame grew, he became a more frequent target of enemy hatchetmen.

The hatchetmen finally caught up with him in 1949. Playing against Rice, Doak was knocked unconscious when he was tackled out of bounds and thrown heavily against the wheelchair of a disabled veteran watching from the sidelines. He was carried from the field, and Rice went on to deal SMU its first defeat in the Southwest Conference since 1946. After the game Walker went to the Rice dressing room to congratulate the players. Among them was the man who had hurled him against the wheelchair. The following summer Doak met another member of the Rice team and said, "How much was the pot of dough you guys had up for me last fall?"

The Rice player shrugged. "We wouldn't do a thing like that, Doak."

"Well," Doak said, "I just was curious to find out how much you guys figured I was worth."

A virus and dysentery kept Walker out of the Kentucky game that fall, and he was in the Texas game barely long enough to kick the extra point which gave SMU a victory, 7-6. He was ill once more before the Mustangs played Texas A&M, but he went out on the field and scored 15 points in a 27-27 tie. He scored three touchdowns against both Arkansas and Baylor, and played magnificently against Texas Christian until he injured his leg in the second half. It was his last college game. When SMU went down gallantly before Notre Dame in their final game of the season, Doak sat on the bench in his street clothes. He had gone as far as he could.

It was the close of the most colorful career any Texas college player has had. So great was his reputation that he was again chosen for the Associated Press All-America team, the first time a player appeared on it three times. The handsome kid with the sandy hair and blue-green eyes had been pictured on dozens of magazine covers and featured in countless newspaper stories. His buildup was the kind that Texans like—big—but there was nothing phony about it. He was equipped with neither a high-pressure publicity man nor a talent for grabbing headlines with his mouth. His publicity was founded only on his marvelous play on the football field. The lessons that his father had taught him as a boy stayed with him; he remembered them when he was off the field as well as in competition. When asked by Bill Rives of the Dallas *Morning News* if he read his press clippings, Doak shook his head. "I don't have to read the paper," he said. "I know what the score was. I played in the game."

Texans were immeasurably proud of their little halfback. They showered him with gifts, pointed him out in the street and were visibly thrilled to shake his hand. Every boy in Dallas wanted to wear the number 37—Doak's number—on the back of his jersey. The children in the Stephan J. Hay School in Dallas made him a study project; to them he was as intriguing as Sam Houston, Davey Crockett or any other Texas hero.

Doak, having gathered all the honors that can come to a college player, might easily have taken the easy way out. There were a number of attractive business offers waiting for him in Dallas, and certainly there were dozens of opportunities for him to go into coaching. In retirement his fame would have been secure. To enter professional football was to jeopardize the reputation painfully constructed through three and a half seasons of college ball. The pros wanted him, of course, because he would be an excellent gate attraction around the league for at least a year. If, as they suspected, he was too small to be a successful player, they would retrieve part of the money they were paying him by exploiting his college reputation.

The pros based their pessimistic estimate of Doak's chances on the theory that he had no single talent of which you could say: "He does this better than anybody else." His coach at SMU, Matty Bell, once said of him, "Doak isn't especially fast. He's not a great kicker. He's not a great passer. He's not a great blocker." And then Bell added: "But he's the greatest football player I have ever seen."

An expert likes to see a quality that he can put his finger on. When looking at a back like Ollie Matson, he can point to his terrific speed; when looking at Alan Ameche he can observe the ferocious power in his legs and shoulders; when looking at Hugh McElhenny he can be enthusiastic over his uncanny skill at dodging tacklers in an open field. The expert becomes confused when he watches a player whose ability is greater than the sum of his talents.

Walker, who never sidestepped a challenge, decided to play pro football. He became the property of the Detroit Lions, a team whose quarterback was Doak's old friend, Bobby Layne. It didn't take Walker long to prove he belonged in the National Football League. In one of the Lions' first exhibition games he went back into punt formation, got a bad pass from center and found himself the target of a handful of onrushing enemy linemen. Doak made a hurried decision. He raced 20 yards to his right and, still running at top speed, punted deep over the heads of the in-drawn enemy defenders.

He took advantage of every asset he had. Because the Lions needed a field-goal kicker Doak took over the job. He had kicked only one field goal in college but he had been a deft place-kicker on points after touchdown. During his rookie season at Detroit he kicked eight field goals. His father had helped him to develop a pair of strong, relaxed hands, ideal for catching a football, and Doak took advantage of this asset to become one of the league's most effective pass receivers. Though he had neither great speed nor power as a runner, he had the knack of gaining the fullest possible protection from his interference.

"Doak's marvelous at picking up his blockers," Buddy

Parker, then Detroit's backfield coach, said. "That takes plenty of poise. If he gets his blockers in front of him, no one can hit him from the front. To get him they have to catch him from behind."

The Lions were quickly rewarded for their faith in Walker. In that memorable debut before the home fans in Detroit, Doak scored all of the Lions' points as they won, 10-7. It was a hint of what was to come. He continued to score points at a rate that startled even his warmest admirers. In one game against the Green Bay Packers he scored three touchdowns and kicked a field goal and three extra points to account for all of Detroit's points. His third touchdown that day brought the Lions from behind with less than two minutes to play. They won, 24-21.

In every game he performed at least one feat which the press could describe as "miraculous." At the end of the season he looked back on an astonishing record. He had scored 11 touchdowns and kicked eight field goals and 36 extra points. His total of 128 points led the league and fell only ten points short of the all-time record which Don Hutson had established in 1942. He was voted "Rookie of the Year," and named a halfback on the league's all-star team. The little guy had not only made good with the pros, he had dazzled them.

There is a postscript to the story. Doak proved his durability as well as his courage by remaining in the league for six seasons. In five of those seasons he was an all-league halfback and, when he retired at the end of 1955 to enter the construction business in Dallas, his total of 534 points was the third highest in the National Football League's history. The determined little halfback seemed to get better as he grew older and he left the league as he had entered it—by winning the scoring championship.

After his final game, Edward J. Anderson, the president of the Lions, ordered that the number 37 which Walker had worn throughout his career be retired from use. "We've never done anything like this before," Anderson said, "but it is a little different in 'The Doaker's' case."

Chapter 10 **The Man of Steel**

When Tony Zale came back to boxing after four years in the Navy, it seemed unlikely that there was in his future anything more than a momentary role as the sacrificial lamb in the exciting drama of Rocky Graziano. This was 1946 and Graziano was the most glamorous figure in the sport. A wildly savage fighter in the ring and a cocky extrovert out of it, Rocky had piled up a series of stunning knockouts. Zale's return was noticed by the public (and Rocky) only because it removed the middleweight championship of the world from the retirement in which it had lingered since Tony had gone into the Navy in 1942. The obscure champion was to act as a foil for the powerful young challenger then moving toward the climactic moment of his career.

Zale, in the advance publicity for the fight, made an ideal foil. He had two assets, one the prestige of holding the middleweight championship, the other a reputation as a solid puncher, which gave him at least an outside chance against Graziano. But other than that he was a dubious attraction for a big outdoor fight. Just before the war he had emerged from a tangle of mediocre middleweights to establish his claim to the title. He had been seen only twice in New York and had given no evidence of the punch which had lifted him to the championship in the West, for he had had to climb off the floor to outpoint light-hitting Georgie Abrams in fifteen rounds and, outweighed by twelve pounds, had been beaten by Billy Conn. Outside of a half-dozen tune up bouts early in 1946 he had not had a fight in four years, an inordinate length of time for any fighter and especially so for one who was thirty-two years old. His previous record, his age and his long inactivity did not speak well for his chances against Graziano. To further damage his chances, Zale got pneumonia while in training for the bout, and it was postponed two months until September 27.

Graziano was six years younger than the champion, had been fighting regularly and combined a deadly punch with a killer instinct which invariably enabled him to finish off his wobbling foes once he had nailed them with his right hand. He was the first "Atomic Puncher," having risen to eminence in the days when his publicists were learning of the events at Hiroshima and Nagasaki, though his admirers who had a taste for alliteration preferred "Rockabye Rocky." He was as talkative as Zale was close-mouthed, as excitable as Zale was phlegmatic. Crowds jammed the gymnasium to see him train, followed him in the streets and shouted and wagered enthusiastically at his fights. He attracted the hordes of hangers-on which had always distinguished the popular fighters of the past and, wherever he went, you would be certain to see around him his old pals from New York's East Side, hoodlums he had met in reform school and a variety of Broadway characters. One steady follower was a little fellow whom Rocky admired as a musician. This fellow played the harmonica, not like ordinary mortals, but by blowing air into it through his nostrils. His repertory was limited to three numbers but one of them, "The Bugle Call Rag," he played while holding the harmonica to his nose with his right hand and saluting with his left.

"Did you ever see anything like that?" Rocky would ask. "I wish I could get this poor guy a job."

When Graziano jogged toward the ring which was pitched on the infield at Yankee Stadium that chilly fall evening he was an 11-5 betting favorite. A deep roar rolled out of the darkness of the stands as he sprang through the ropes, his silver robe, trimmed in green and red, flapping behind him. The flamboyant Rocky had lured most of that crowd of 40,000 people to the Stadium, a larger crowd than that which had watched the great Joe Louis knock out Tami Mauriello in New York only nine days before. Graziano jogged in his corner to stay warm, occasionally stamping and pawing the ground like an impatient bull, anxious to get at his foe. His unruly black curly hair emphasized the wild streak in him.

In a moment Zale was in the ring, too, climbing in less ostentatiously, and drawing less attention and applause. He wore gray flannel slacks under his white robe and sat quietly in his corner. His broad face was pale and impassive, and his thin blond hair neatly parted and slicked down. Referee Ruby Goldstein called the fighters to the center of the ring for their instructions, then they touched gloves in an almost unconscious gesture which passed for a handshake, and in another few seconds the bell rang to begin one of the most memorable prize fights of all time.

Zale moved across the ring and fired his best weapon at Rocky, smashing right hands to the body. Graziano fought back, rocking Zale with a right-hand punch to the head, then driving him into the ropes. The champion got under most of his punches and Rocky missed wildly. Zale, the cooler of the two, found an opening and drove a right uppercut, then a short left hook, to Graziano's chin, dropping him for a count of four. When he got up, Rocky seemed scornful of Zale's punches and, rushing furiously in, caught the surprised champion with three powerful right hands that drew blood from Tony's mouth and sent him wobbling to his corner at the end of the round.

Zale's chance for victory seemed to have flitted by. Rocky was eager to get at him as the second round began and a couple of his crushing right hands drew the life from Tony's legs and made him an easy target. Rocky hammered him about the head and the blood ran in little streams down his bony face. The skin seemed drawn tighter across his face now and it was yellow under the glare of the lights, giving it the appearance of a death's head. His body sagged under the punches of his wild-eyed opponent, and he crumpled to the floor under a clublike right. His pale blue eyes staring vacantly at the crowd, his mouth hanging open, Zale clutched at a strand of the ropes and pulled himself to his feet at the count of four. The bell rang to give him a merciful minute of rest.

The sickening brutality of the third round was relieved only by Zale's obstinate courage. He took a fearful beating around the head, but stood up under Graziano's relentless fists, occasionally trying to stand off the challenger with a right hand which had been broken in the second round. Zale was turned partly around by the force of one of Rocky's blows and sent reeling into the ropes. Moving in quickly, Graziano grabbed

Zale's puffed, bleeding face with his left glove and hammered it relentlessly with his right. But for the heartless code of the ring which decrees that a champion be allowed to keep fighting while even the slimmest hope remains to him, the fight would have been stopped there. Instead, Zale endured his agony until the bell sent him lurching to his corner on legs that appeared to crumble under him at every step.

Zale astonished and thrilled the crowd by fighting back strongly in the fourth round. Perhaps Graziano had wearied himself by the fury of his own attack; perhaps Tony had hurt him with his own punishing blows to the body. Zale landed one of those body punches and Rocky's knee convulsively jerked up. A left hook brought blood trickling from the challenger's nose. But at the bell Rocky was throwing his wild rights again and the crowd believed it had seen a last-ditch effort by a gallant fighter.

It seemed a certainty in the fifth round. Rocky, cooler now and sensing victory, measured Zale for his devastating punches and almost took the old champion's head off his shoulders with a couple of them. Zale wearily fought back, but was repeatedly beaten to the punch by the younger man. The sole consolation for Zale's friends was that he probably knew little of what was going on. He remained upright only by instinct.

As the sixth round began there were cries of "Stop the fight!" from those in the crowd who felt the champion was in danger of being seriously hurt. Zale walked out, his legs steadier now, and threw punches at Graziano. Rocky rallied, throwing punches of his own at Zale's body. One stopped Tony in his tracks and a look of pain lit up for a brief moment his dull blue eyes. He crouched and moved away. Rocky still plodded forward, trying to put over the one punch under which Zale must finally come apart. And then, in a moment, it was all over. Zale jabbed a straight left to Graziano's face and drove a right hand under his heart. Rocky hung there an instant, as if impaled on Zale's arm. Then he crumpled and Zale hit him on the chin with a left hook as he went down.

Paralyzed by the body blow, Graziano groped desperately for the strand of rope by which he might pull himself to his feet. The crowd, stunned for a moment by the sudden and unbelievable turn of events, then came alive in a deafening roar. Rocky thrashed feebly on the canvas, tried again for the strand of rope and then gaped at Goldstein in despair as the referee counted "Eight-nine-ten!"

The champion, his face slashed, his right hand broken and his brain temporarily clouded, was helped to his dressing room. The crowd, the press, even cynical old-time boxing men, were elated at what they knew was one of the most gallant stands a fighter had ever made. There were others, many of them disgruntled bettors, who were not as enthusiastic about Graziano's performance.

"Graziano got hit in the belly," somebody said, "and he quit like a dog."

But Izzy Kline, one of Zale's handlers, had an answer for that. "I hear some people claim Rocky dogged it," Izzy said. "But those people never got hit in the gut by Tony Zale."

Kline, like the rest of the men who knew Zale, did not share in the general wonder at his incredible stand against Graziano. Those close to him were aware that he never would have won the championship in the first place had he not been born with more than his share of courage, for the road he traveled to Yankee Stadium had carried him through enough batterings and heartaches to break a lesser man. His nickname, "The

Man of Steel," was more than just an allusion to the steel mills of his home town, Gary, Indiana. He was a hard man, both in body and determination.

Surely there was nothing soft in his background. Born Anthony Florian Zaleski on May 29, 1914, the son of a steel worker, he lived his childhood on the edge of poverty. When he was two years old his father was killed by a car which crashed into the bicycle he was riding. Tony's three older brothers went to work in the mills to hold the family together and later Tony, growing to manhood during the Depression, joined them there. All of the brothers liked to box and Tony got his first lessons (and lickings) from his older brother, John. At sixteen he won his first Golden Gloves championship (welterweight) in Gary, and won again in 1931 and 1933 and won the middleweight title in 1934. The result of this last victory was an unexpected trip to New York. The Chicago Golden Gloves team was about to leave for Madison Square Garden to battle the New York team when its light heavyweight representative, an unknown Negro boy named Joe Louis, was declared ineligible. It seems that Louis belonged to the Detroit team, not Chicago's. Zale, though only a middleweight, was thought to be the best replacement available. He went to Madison Square Garden, gave away at least ten pounds to his opponent, and lost. He would not have been quite so discouraged that evening if he had known that his opponent, Melio Bettina, was to go on to win the light heavyweight championship of the world.

When he returned to Gary in June, Zale became a professional fighter. He had lost only eight of his ninety-five amateur fights, he knew he could punch and he believed he would pick up as he went along the skills that a fighter needs for success.

It was a disillusioning experience. Boxing has always been infested by men who are willing to manage and "train" fighters,
while they are unwilling or unable to teach them how to protect themselves. They live by the blood and sweat of sturdy
young men. Within ten weeks Zale was promoted from four-
round bouts to eight rounders. Within six months he was
struggling to keep his head above water in ten-round bouts,
against experienced professionals. Every bout was a brawl.
Sometimes he won, sometimes he lost, but the human body
was not designed for such wear and tear. In May, 1935, he was
knocked out in six rounds by Johnny Phagan. Tony tried again
in July and was beaten by Dave Clark. In a little over one year
he had fought twenty-eight times, mostly in Chicago, and
had lost twelve fights. He had been cut and bruised and now
an injury to his side gave him intense pain even when he
trained. Discouraged, and with little money to show for his
suffering, he returned to Gary and took a job in a steel mill.

"I never really gave up hope that someday I'd be a good
fighter," Zale was to say later. "But I realized that I wasn't
learning anything and I was getting hurt."

Sniping cinders in front of an open hearth in a big mill is not
the most pleasant refuge in the world, even for a man who had
absorbed as many beatings as Zale. The great furnaces sap the
youth from a man and leave him dry and old. But, aside from
fighting, it was all Zale knew. "I kept in shape," Zale said. "I
worked out in a gym fairly often, not so much because I
wanted to go back to fighting in a hurry, but because I felt
better when I worked out. And sniping cinders keeps you in
shape, too. But too much of it will bring a man down."

All the while there burned in Zale, as real to him as the tormenting heat of the hearths, a desire to return to boxing. The torn muscles in his side had long since healed, and he could do the heaviest work without a trace of pain. In July, 1937, just one month after that same Joe Louis whom he had replaced on the 1934 Golden Gloves team had won the heavyweight championship of the world, Zale returned to the ring. His two years in the mills had toughened his body and given him an added incentive to make good in boxing.

He was a better fighter this time, and his record improved. He started at the very bottom again, in four rounders, and won eight out of nine fights as he progressed to eight rounders. And then, in a fight with Jimmy Clark, he was nailed with a solid punch early in the first round, couldn't shake it off and lost by a knockout when the referee stopped the fight. It began to appear that his return to the steel mills was inevitable.

One day in the spring of 1938 a small-time Chicago promoter, Benny Ray, paid a visit to his friends, Sam Pian and Art Winch. Pian and Winch formed a successful manager-trainer partnership in Chicago. It was under their guidance that Barney Ross had won the lightweight and welterweight titles. Ray thought he saw a way to repay them for several favors they had done him in the past.

"There's a kid fighting in the small clubs around here that I think you'd be interested in," Ray said. "His name is Zale and he's green as hell, and he's been punched down and around, but he's a real good puncher himself. If you could teach him something he could make a lot of money for himself, and for you, too."

By this time Zale's contract had passed into the hands of his brother, John. Winch went to see Tony, and liked what he saw. "I liked him as soon as I talked to him," Winch said later. "He wasn't one of them fresh kids who knows everything.

So we gave his brother $200 for the contract, and began to teach Zale how to fight."

The raw material was there—a finely conditioned and eager young man, weighing 160 pounds and possessing a paralyzing punch. Zale learned painfully slowly, but his career progressed more quickly than his new managers had expected; he was able to rectify a multitude of technical sins with one crushing punch. One of his most satisfying victories was a two-round knockout of Jimmy Clark, the man who had stopped him in the first round only a few months before. Near the end of 1939 he scored five straight quick knockouts and looked so impressive that Pian and Winch were convinced that he was ready to fight any middleweight in the country.

The opportunity for Zale to confirm their belief came unexpectedly. Pian was watching Zale work out in the gym one day, marveling to himself how a fighter could box so ineptly in a workout, as Zale always did, and yet be so dangerous in a real fight. He was joined by Nate Druxman, a Seattle promoter whom he had known for some years. Druxman handled the affairs of Al Hostak, who was then the middleweight champion and whom Jack Dempsey had once called the hardest puncher he had ever seen below the heavyweight division.

"We're bringing Hostak to Cleveland for a fight," Druxman said to Pian, "and we'd like to show him in Chicago, too. Do you have a boy he could box here?"

Pian did his best to remain unconcerned while keeping his heart out of his mouth. This was the match he was looking for. He was certain that if he could lure the unsuspecting champion to Chicago Zale would have a good chance against him. He felt that the rugged Zale could stand up under Hostak's best punches and that the champion would wilt under

Tony's relentless body attack. "Well," Pian said, "I got this kid Zale that's in the ring now. He's got a following around Chicago, and I think he and Hostak would draw pretty good."

Druxman frowned. "He don't look so good to me," he said, "and as I remember his record isn't so good, either. You got anybody else?"

"He's all I got," Pian said.

And so Druxman, assured by Pian that Zale was not likely to die in the ring, and yet pleased at the prospect of a soft fight and a profitable evening for his fighter, agreed to bring Hostak to Chicago for a non-title bout. Tony, on the eve of his big chance, could not shake the gremlins which so often appeared at crucial moments of his career. A siege of the flu caused the fight to be postponed for two weeks. When he entered the ring on January 29, 1940, to face the champion, he was pale and sluggish, and events in the early rounds led the fans to believe they would see a quick knockout.

Hostak fired a barrage of punches in the first round, but found himself thwarted by the same unyielding chin which Graziano was to encounter more than six years later. Zale rocked and wavered but never crumbled. Hostak remained in command through the first four rounds, picking his openings and firing his heavy punches through them. Zale stood up under everything he threw. In the fifth round, having been urged by his handlers to attack Hostak's body, Zale turned the tide with a punishing right under the heart. He pressed his advantage, sent Hostak reeling under another right hand to the chin, and dominated the rest of the fight. He was awarded the unanimous decision.

After the fight Hostak announced that he had broken his right hand. "Maybe so," shrugged Winch, "but Tony broke his heart."

So convincing had Zale's triumph been that he was signed for a title bout with Hostak in the champion's home town, Seattle. Pian and Winch, confident that a healthy Zale would knock out Hostak the next time they fought, did not worry about a close decision going in favor of the home-town favorite. Zale did everything expected of him. He gave one of the most ferocious exhibitions of body punching that this "head-hunting" age of boxing has seen, knocked Hostak down three times and won the middleweight championship by stopping him in the thirteenth round. The date was July 19, 1940.

There was a year and a half left to him before he went into the Navy, not time enough, as it turned out, for him to win recognition as an outstanding fighter. He was not even considered the world champion in New York at this time, because the boxing commission of that state, at odds with the National Boxing Association, had crowned its own champion. After his victory over Hostak, Zale lost a non-title bout to Billy Soose in Chicago. Soose, a tall slender boy who later held briefly the New York version of the championship, was in trouble in the first round, but then managed to evade Zale's best punches and won the decision.

"But Tony almost finished me with one punch in the first," Soose said afterward. "He hit me in the belly and it felt like somebody had stuck a red hot poker in there."

Then Zale went through 1941 unbeaten, knocking out Hostak again, this time after having him down seven times in the second round, and finally earned even New York's approval as champion by beating clever Georgie Abrams in fifteen rounds. For his last fight before going in the Navy, Tony was matched with Billy Conn, the former light heavyweight champion who had just made a spectacular run at Joe Louis. The match seems to have been made because Conn's handlers wanted to earn the kind of money they could get only from having him meet a "name" fighter, yet they did not want to have him deprived of a return bout with Louis by being beaten. Zale, of course, had no chance against Conn, by then a heavyweight, but he accepted the assignment without complaint and made an interesting fight of it. Conn was awarded the decision.

This, then, was the fighter who came back after the war and astonished all those who knew him only by what they had read about him. Zale had put new life into boxing with his bravery and power, wiping out the bad taste left by the Louis-Conn fiasco earlier that summer, and thrilling millions of people who had never even seen a prize fight. The plans for a return bout with Graziano in New York were ruined by Rocky's suspension in that state, a suspension that turned out to be prompted more by the desire of a number of politicians to get their names in the paper than by the presence of a sound case against the New York slugger. Rocky was barred (1) for refusing to report a bribe (which may never have been offered him) to throw a fight (which never took place) and (2) for several offenses he committed while in the Army and for which he had already been punished. The fight, then, was held in Chicago, on July 16, 1947.

It is a generally accepted theory in boxing that, once two men have fought a rousing battle, the return match is a dull one. It has happened often in the past, but it did not happen in the second fight between Zale and Graziano. It matched their first brawl in savagery and excitement. The evening would have been memorable if for nothing else than the heat inside Chicago Stadium, for the temperature rose to 120 degrees. It was an exhausting effort to move in such a monstrous oven; to stand up under fearful punishment and keep fighting back for six rounds seemed beyond human endurance. And yet that is what Zale and Graziano did.

The course of the fight in Chicago differed from that of their first one. Zale battered Graziano in the early rounds, putting him down and closing his right eye with a series of deadly punches. Rocky, fiercely resenting the charges that his courage had not matched Zale's in their first bout, flew back at the champion in rages that were all the more frustrating because he couldn't see him. Blood poured into his left eye and his right appeared hopelessly closed. Then, between the fourth and fifth rounds, Graziano's handlers, resorting to primitive surgery, pressed the edge of a quarter against the eyelid, breaking the skin, and with it the swelling which had caused the eye to close. Rocky, given new life, hurled himself at Zale in the fifth round, got in some solid punches and came out for the sixth far the stronger of the two. The intense heat, his age and the brutal assault of Graziano had left Zale defenseless, open to the murderous blows of one of the hardest punchers the ring has known. Rocky hammered Zale across the ring, raining lefts and rights on his head and body, driving Tony along the ropes before him, sometimes turning him completely around with the force of his punches. But "The Man of Steel" would not go down. It was the referee, not Graziano, who finally ended the slaughter, raising Rocky's hand in victory.

"I wanted to kill him," Graziano said in his dressing room a few minutes later. "I got nothing against him. He's a nice guy. I like him, but I wanted to kill him."

These two brave men were now irrevocably locked in the most brutal series in the history of the most brutal of all sports. The demand for a third bout, one which would settle the issue once and for all, began almost as soon as the beaten Zale had been helped to his corner. Boxing men were almost unanimous in their opinion that Zale had little chance in a third bout with Graziano. Thirty-three-year-old men do not recover from a beating like that which Tony had taken. Graziano, the younger man, would have everything in his favor from now on. But Pian and Winch, like Zale, believed in Tony's ability to come back and regain his title. There was no doubt in anybody's mind about Zale's courage, and the veteran fighter also had on his side the wonderful body which he had taken such care to condition.

"You can hardly tell, the way Tony lives, whether he's training for a fight or not," Winch said. "He don't smoke or drink, he eats only one good meal a day and even then he is very careful what he eats. You bring him to New York for a party like the Boxing Writers' Dinner, and where do you find him in the afternoon? In Stillman's Gymnasium, where he is punching the bag, skipping the rope and shadow boxing. So when it comes to training for a fight, the only difference is he boxes with his sparring partners every day."

Zale was ready for the third bout with Graziano. Sure that the terrible heat in Chicago Stadium, rather than Rocky's fists, had finally brought about his defeat, Tony looked eagerly toward this chance to redeem himself and win back the middleweight championship. They fought in Newark, New Jersey, on June 10, 1948, and Rocky never had a chance. Zale attacked from the opening bell, keeping him off balance with stiff jabs and looking for the openings he knew the wild-swinging Rocky would give him. Graziano, fighting back, presented Zale his opening, and in a moment he was on the floor, knocked there by a left hook and a right cross.

What was left of that first round was as wild as anything that had gone on in their first two fights. They tore at each other savagely, pouring on punches as if they were determined that only one of them would walk out of that ring alive. When the bell rang to end the round neither man heard it and they flailed away until pried apart by the referee. Zale frustrated Rocky's rushes in the second round, pulling away from his roundhouse rights and driving home powerful punches of his own. Graziano brought the crowd to its feet for a moment when he landed one of his famous right hands on Zale's chin, but Tony shook it off and was battering the champion at the bell.

The fight ended in the third round. Zale's numbing body punches immobilized Rocky almost as completely as if he had torn off his legs. Two hard lefts sent Rocky down for a count of seven and when he climbed to his feet he wobbled badly. Zale ducked a couple of his wild rights, then placed a series of vicious punches to Graziano's head and sent him crashing unconscious to the floor.

"Do you think there'll be a fourth fight?" a reporter asked a happy Zale afterward in his dressing room.

"I've had three helpings of Rocky," Tony grinned. "Now let someone else have him for a change."

Neither fighter was quite the same after the ordeal of their three battles. Zale lost his championship to Marcel Cerdan later that summer and retired; the younger Graziano fought, with varying success, for four more years. But the story that they acted out mercilessly and courageously will be told as long as people believe two men can prove their worth by meeting in combat. Of the two, Tony Zale's accomplishment was the greater. His name has ever since remained a symbol of the finest kind of courage in the ring.

Chapter 11 The Hawk They Couldn't Kill

"I won't know until I play whether I can get back the edge I had before. I don't know if I'll start favoring a shoulder or an ankle that's paining me and then throw my game off. But there's one thing I'm sure of. There's nothing about death that will ever frighten me now."

Pain had torn at the little man for months and death had made a run at him and the hard lines in his face had been etched there as if by acid. The Texas sun had tanned him, but his gaunt, still-handsome face reflected his ordeal just as surely as did the scars on his body. His jacket hung slackly on him, making him look like a small boy in a big brother's coat and underscoring his frailness. The laces of his G.I. boots were loosened at the tops to ease the pressure on his swollen ankles. Yet in his eyes there was neither despair nor desperation. There was the same icy stare which was the outward manifestation of the most indomitable spirit golf has known, the look which had chilled his competitors as he drove himself to the top of his profession and had helped to earn him that scarcely endearing nickname, "The Hawk."

It was the summer of 1949 and Ben Hogan sat in the living room of his home in Fort Worth. The friend who had come expecting to see a hopeless invalid—to view, as it were, the mortal remains of the greatest golfer of his time—abruptly lost the feeling that he was there to offer Ben or anyone else his condolences. As Hogan talked of his hopes and his plans for the future in the same intense way he approached a ball in a difficult lie, taking nothing for granted yet determined not to fail because of anything over which he had control, the visitor began to absorb his confidence. When the man left he took with him, as did others who visited Hogan at that time, a conviction that he might yet live to see a miracle.

If only men of superior faith can believe in miracles, it must be said that, where Hogan was concerned, most of the country's sports fans were infidels. The terrible highway accident which shattered the little golf champion's body and the even more ravaging complications which followed a month later must surely have put an end to his career. Most of his friends were grateful that he was still alive. They looked forward to the day when he could join them on the veranda of one of the country clubs he had once conquered and, perhaps, at some distant date, even hit a few balls in a friendly foursome. They remembered the reports from the scene of the accident, how a giant bus had roared down on the Hogan car, plowed into it head-on and squashed it as a stampeding elephant would mangle a small animal that had wandered into its path.

Yet, even as they consigned him to the graveyard of champions and debated the identity of his successor as the country's finest golfer, Hogan was slowly conditioning himself for what was to be the most incredible comeback in the history of American sports. The doctors had mended his shattered bones and tied up his torn veins; now it was up to him to strengthen his muscles, regain his co-ordination and bring under control the nerves which had carried him to the top in the most nerveracking of all games. At the age of thirty-seven he was faced with the task of rebuilding what had been a nearly flawless golfing machine. To understand the magnitude of that task, remember that Bobby Jones, the sport's most famous player before Hogan, had retired from competitive golf at twenty-eight.

But William Benjamin Hogan seemed to have been put on this earth for the purpose of hurdling obstacles. Looking back now on his career, it can be said that Hogan first overcame the greatest handicap any athlete can have—no talent. That deficiency alone was enough to endear him to millions of duffers. Though born in Dublin, Texas, a son of the village blacksmith, on August 13, 1912, Ben spent most of his boyhood in Fort Worth, where his mother had moved the family after his father's death. In common with so many other great athletes, he lived his early years in poverty. When he grew up the memory of those lean days still haunted him and added its weight to the desperate hunger for victory which we associate with him. He sold papers for a time but, hearing that caddies were paid sixty-five cents an hour, plus tips, he applied for a job at one of the city's finest golf courses, the Glen Garden Country Club.

The skinny, underfed little Hogan, only twelve years old,

had his first battle on his hands. He was a natural mark for the older, bigger boys. He had only been at work a day or two when his "colleagues" stuffed him into a frail barrel and rolled him down a hill. Having survived that ordeal with little damage except to his dignity, he was forced to fight one of the other caddies. Hogan, who even today looks as if he would have made a champion boxer, sailed into his unlucky opponent and proved himself with his fists.

There was another battle that was not to be won so easily. As they made their living from golf, all of the caddies wanted to be able to play the game, too, and they spent their spare hours practicing driving and putting. And, as all boys do, they made even their practice sessions a form of competition. The boy who hit the shortest drive was forced to retrieve the balls for the other caddies. Ben was small and skinny; he was left-handed and there were only right-handed clubs available for him at the club; and so he became the regular retriever for his colleagues.

It was here that Hogan formulated what has since become his motto, the true secret of his success: "If you can't outplay them, outwork them." Though worn out from hauling heavy bags of clubs over the rolling course all day, he stayed there after the others had gone home and worked long hours at the practice tee. Slowly he began to feel that hitting a ball right-handed was the natural way. Slowly he began to get the distance on his drives that would end his days as a "retriever" for the other caddies. This was the origin of his powerful backswing, the mighty effort which was to propel the longest drives any little man has ever hit on a golf course.

"There is no such thing as a natural swing," Hogan has often said, and the young Ben Hogan was certainly the living

proof of that conviction. Veteran golfers who watched the
little fellow on the course were impressed by his determination but appalled by his form. One friend from those days
still carries a vivid picture in his mind of the clumsy beginner.
"He couldn't do one thing right. He sure couldn't putt.
Everybody used to laugh at him because he practically ran
at the ball to hit it."

But Hogan loved golf and he saw in it a way out of the
poverty which had darkened all of his early life. He had
neither the size nor the natural talent. Such considerations
were as nothing to a man with Ben's fierce singleness of purpose. He worked and worked on his game and soon he was
beating most of the other young men around Fort Worth.
He stopped growing when he reached five feet, eight and a
half inches and 140 pounds. Yet out of such refractory material was evolving a fine golfer—one good enough to leave
Fort Worth and hit the tournament trail. Or so he thought.

The few dollars in his pockets couldn't carry him very far.
There was little chance to win any real money against the
tough veterans of the tournament circuit then, and Ben was
usually forced to return to Fort Worth and earn his living
with any one of a half-dozen jobs. And, in 1935, he married
his childhood sweetheart, Valerie Fox. Knowing how much
he loved the game, Valerie urged him to go back to the golf
circuit, feeling that he was now ready to compete with the
old pros. Ben thought so, too. "When I made the tour before,"
he told a friend some years later, "I'd have an occasional good
round, but I couldn't keep it up. One good shot or one good
round doesn't mean a thing in this game. You've got to keep
it up for seventy-two holes."

Ben and Valerie set out together in 1937. He had never

won a tournament, and there were times when it appeared that he never would. Everything seemed to go against him. In 1938 the Hogans drove their battered jalopy into Oakland for a tournament and, because they couldn't afford a parking lot, left the car in a vacant lot. He played badly in the tournament, winning but a few dollars, and when they got back to the lot they found that the car had been jacked up by thieves and stripped of its tires.

"You might say that that was a break for me," Ben will tell you. "I knew then that things couldn't get much worse for us. And Valerie, who must have figured I was beginning to lose heart, pretended she was more optimistic than ever."

Things did take a turn for the better. There were no tournament victories, but he gave the winner a run for it almost every time. In fact, he was beginning to finish second with such regularity that he earned for himself the nickname, "Runner-Up Hogan." Anyone who has ever met him can tell you how much that name must have rankled him.

Through it all he worked harder than any other man in golf. "I never heard of a harder worker in golf or any other sport," Bobby Jones once said of him. He had mastered nearly every shot now except the putt, and that was costing him tournaments.

"I used to feel sorry for the little guy," Jimmy Demaret, the colorful pro, says. "Imagine anybody feeling sorry for Hogan now! I get tired of seeing his rear end and his elbows when he bends down to pick the ball out of the cup. But then it just seemed that he *never* was going to learn to putt."

Nineteen forty was his year. He finished second in his first six tournaments, meanwhile keeping Valerie awake at night as he practiced putting on the rug in their hotel rooms. It had been eight years since he first set out on the tour in 1932. When he finally broke through, winning the Pinehurst North & South Open, he was on his way to greatness. He just kept winning. By the end of the year he was golf's biggest money winner. Again in 1941 and 1942 he was the leading money winner in the country and he was acclaimed the finest golfer in the world.

And then, when he had perfected his marvelous style, the bottom dropped out of his world, just as it did for so many other people. World War II had reached America and Ben was off to join the Air Corps. He returned after the war and regained his peak much more quickly than most of his colleagues did. He was working as hard as ever. At the top of his game in 1947 he was audacious enough to alter his golfing style, having learned to control his hook by fading the ball. And in 1948 he accomplished the unprecedented feat of sweeping the U.S. Open (his first), the Western Open and the PGA tournament.

To win the U.S. Open he had to top a magnificent performance by his old friend Demaret. Jimmy had finished with a score of 278, an all-time low for the Open. "But I knew I didn't have this tournament won," Demaret recalls. "I knew that Hogan was going great, too, and so I sat on the clubhouse veranda to watch him come in. Then I saw him walking down the eighteenth fairway and I knew my goose was cooked. His head was so low he looked like a gopher climbing out of a hole. When Ben walks like that you know there's nothing going to stop him. I just began figuring out what I was going to do with my second-place money."

Demaret knew what he was talking about. Ben finished with a new record of 276 and captured the Open title.

He was now in a class by himself, but there was always his obsession to improve on perfection. "It takes him three hours to play nine holes in practice," one of his caddies said. "He'll make me drop a dozen or so balls in a sand trap and then he'll go down there and blast every darn one of them out. Then, like as not, he'll knock another dozen out of there."

A reporter once asked Hogan if he ever relaxed on the course. A look of genuine astonishment crossed his face. "Relax? How can anybody relax and play golf? You have to grip the club, don't you?"

Every other golfer in the business realized what Demaret meant when he said that he knew, after one look at Hogan, that he had no chance to win the 1949 Open. A group stood around the fifteenth green at a tournament one day and watched another famous golfer line up a putt. It was a tournament which Hogan had not entered. "Look at that fellow," one of the group said. "He's as calm as can be out there. I even saw him grinning a few minutes ago. But if Hogan was in this tournament you'd see this guy shake when he lit his cigarette. He's got ulcers, and do you know who gave them to him? Ben Hogan."

There was something menacing about Hogan in his prime. He chose his club and strode toward the ball with all the grim purposefulness of an executioner approaching his grisly job. Standing over the ball, his knees loose, his butt out, his toes pointing outward, at a slight angle, he was an extraordinary symbol of the great athlete about to spring into action. That stance foretold the powerful, beautifully coordinated swing and the graceful follow-through. It sprang out inevitably, like the bright spectacular patterns from a Chinese firecracker.

Nineteen forty-nine promised to be another brilliant year for Ben. He began by winning the Bing Crosby Invitational and the Long Beach Open, then lost in a play-off to Demaret at Phoenix. Most of the golfers were pushing on to Tucson, but Ben decided to pass up the tournament there and go home for a brief rest before setting out again in quest of the season's more important prizes. Many of his friends urged him to reconsider and go to Tucson.

"No, I want the rest," he told them. "It isn't the golf that wears you out, it's the traveling. I want to die an old man, not a young one."

Less than twenty-four hours later he lay near death in an El Paso hospital.

It was early in the morning of February 2. Ben and Valerie were driving toward Fort Worth on Highway 80, a straight, flat road which stretched interminably across the desolate west Texas prairie. They drove through an early-morning brightness and frequent patches of thick fog which had descended on them. Then they drove for miles wrapped in the fog, the climbing sun only occasionally showing wanly through the murky wall. Ben switched on his headlights. Sometimes the ghost of a car would take form ahead, become palpable only as it reached them, and then fade again into the fog behind. Ben slowed his car to thirty miles an hour. Peering through the windshield he detected two luminous circles coming toward him. He crept closer to the right side of the road. And then the two circles became four and were right on top of him. Out of the fog rushed a mountain of a bus, passing a six-wheeler truck, and Hogan, kept on the road by the culvert to his right, didn't have a chance in the world.

"I put my head down and dived across Valerie like I was diving into a pool of water."

That reflexive action saved both of their lives. The shuddering impact hurled part of the engine back into the driver's seat and demolished the car. Valerie, suffering cuts and bruises, had been saved by her husband's protecting body. She pulled the crushed little champion from his car. Hogan lay there by the roadside for well over an hour as, in the confusion, each bystander thought the other had called an ambulance.

"I thought he was dying," one witness said later. "He just got grayer and grayer."

Finally an ambulance arrived from the nearby town of Van Horn and carried Hogan to a hospital in El Paso, 119 miles away. There the doctors recorded his more serious injuries: a fractured pelvis, a broken left collarbone, a broken left ankle and a chipped rib. The extent of his internal injuries was not to be realized until a month later.

The blood clot that threatened to choke off his life suddenly developed early in March. It came just at a time when the doctors believed Ben was on the way back to health. Moving up his left leg, the clot appeared headed for his heart. The doctors in El Paso thinned Ben's blood and sent for Dr. Alton S. Ochsner, a famous New Orleans surgeon. Because there was difficulty in arranging the surgeon's air passage from New Orleans to El Paso, Hogan's friends finally had him picked up in an Air Force bomber.

When Ochsner arrived, he found the golfer in critical condition. Hogan's blood count was dangerously low, and the clot seemed deadly. He was immediately given a blood transfusion. In a two hour abdominal operation, Ochsner tied off the vena cava, a large vein which feeds blood into the right auricle of the heart. There were serious doubts about Ben's survival and one major news service sent out an up-to-date obituary of him, ready to be put into type when the reporters keeping the "death watch" at the hospital flashed the signal.

The obituary's only possible use came a little over a year later when it might have been valuable in throwing together a biography of Hogan in his hour of triumph. From the moment he began to shake off the dulling effects of the operation, Ben was on the road back to the top of the golf world. He seemed not to care, or even to be aware, that so many knowledgeable people were saying that he would never again play tournament golf.

Two weeks later he was being wheeled about the hospital's grounds to soak up the warm Texas sun. Soon he was out of the hospital and back in his own home in Fort Worth. There were long hours of massage and then the first halting steps as he learned to walk again. When this obstacle was past, he began taking short walks around his bedroom. Later he jogged up and down on the living-room rug, strengthening the muscles in his legs and at the same time squeezing in his hand a rubber ball in an effort to regain his powerful grip. Finally there were long walks around the block, walks that sometimes stretched out so that a worried Valerie drove through the neighboorhood looking for him. And almost everywhere he went he carried with him a golf club, partly because he wanted to get the feel of it in his hands again and partly because he often needed it to rest on. Friends who feared that he was pushing himself too fast invariably got this answer:

"There's no point in just getting up and standing," Ben would tell them. "I've got to walk to get back in shape. I just walk as far as I can and then I lie down and rest."

Nemesis itself must grow weary of pursuing a man like that.

There came inevitably the day when Hogan took his clubs and went out to the golf course. He could play only a few holes and he brought a chair with him so that he could occasionally stop to rest. The damage to his veins had affected the circulation of his blood, and his legs and feet were badly swollen after even the least exertion. And then a curious thing happened. As Ben's strength and stamina returned, so did his marvelous co-ordination. He was amazed to find that, after an eight-month break, his golf game was rapidly returning to what it had been before the accident.

When asked if he planned to go back to competitive golf, Hogan gave his interviewers an honest answer. "There's a good possibility," he said, "but right now I can't say for sure. I'll just have to wait and see how I'm feeling and how my game shapes up. But there's one thing I can say for sure: I'm not going out there and shoot in the eighties."

By then Hogan must have felt fairly certain that he could play golf as well as he ever had. What worried him was the condition of his legs. Would they stand up for a grueling eighteen holes? Or, even worse, the thirty-six holes that he would sometimes have to play in one day? He didn't wait very long to put himself to a test. In January, 1950, less than a year after his accident, Hogan entered the Los Angeles Open. Nobody, of course, expected him to make any kind of a showing. This was just a warmup, a dress rehearsal for the big tournaments of the future. Many of the onlookers believed that Hogan wouldn't even be able to finish the seventy-two-hole tournament over the rugged Riviera Club course.

Then Hogan began to play and it suddenly seemed that he had never been away at all. He almost dominated the field and,

on the verge of winning off by himself, he was overhauled on
the final day when Slammin' Sammy Snead turned in one of
the most brilliant rounds of his career. The two old rivals had
finished in a tie. Hogan (or, more accurately, Hogan's legs)
weren't quite ready for the extra round of golf required for
the play-off, and Snead walked off with the title. Yet this had
been a minor miracle. Hogan was back on the tour and he was
a threat to every golfer in the land.

"Losing that play-off was one of the best breaks I ever got,"
Ben said later. "My game had rounded into shape so easily that
I was getting cocky about it. I might have begun taking my
comeback less seriously. I might have let down."

No one who knows Hogan could take that last remark seriously. Whenever he picked up a golf club, the little champion
became all business, an attitude which led him into many mis-
understandings throughout the great days of his career. Reporters, fans, even his colleagues in professional golf, were
frequently irritated by what they considered Hogan's rude-
ness, aloofness or insatiable greed. In each case the "misunder-
standing" could be traced directly to Ben's almost demonic
craving for victory—a craving which made him so intent on
the course that he often neglected the niceties which the public
expects from its heroes.

As the 1950 U.S. Open, the year's biggest tournament, drew
closer, Hogan was on better terms with the press than ever
before. The writers, aware of the awesome demands he was
making on himself, were openly rooting for him to make a successful comeback and were more than willing to forget their
past differences with him. Hogan, too, was ready to bury the
hatchet. He had only one complaint. With the Open approaching, he wanted the newspapermen to treat him as a golfer, not

as a cripple; he wanted them to write about the tournament, not his aching legs. In reply to one question he snapped:

"It doesn't make any difference how my legs are doing. I'm hurting all over and, damn it, these legs have got to take it just the same as I'm doing."

But whether Ben liked it or not, people were talking about his legs and his courageous attempt to win back the Open title. Adding spice to his quest was his impressive showing in the tournament at Los Angeles. Though it hardly seemed likely that he could make a serious run at the Open title, his earlier performance had created the notion in people's minds that he would cause some excitement at Ardmore, Pennsylvania, where the Open was to be played. It was a wonderful thought.

The greatest golfers in the country descended on the Merion Country Club at Ardmore on Thursday, June 8, for the start of the 1950 Open. The course was one of the toughest on the entire circuit, with treacherous stretches of rough bordering its narrow fairways. To these natural hazards was added the huge gallery which followed Hogan and clogged the fairways. The weather was unseasonably hot at Ardmore and fans who trouped the entire eighteen holes were weary and soaked with perspiration when they finally made their way back to the clubhouse.

Most of the excitement that first day centered around Lee Mackey, Jr., an obscure young pro from Birmingham, Alabama, who fired an astounding 64. Hogan shot a 72, two over par and good enough to place him well up among the leaders. On Friday Hogan came back with a brilliant 69 to move within two strokes of Dutch Harrison, who had taken over the lead from Mackey. That unfortunate young man, whose record-breaking performance had made him a hero only the day before, shot a dismal 81 and dropped completely out of the running.

Hogan could not be overlooked now, but the odds were against him. The tournament was scheduled to end on Saturday with thirty-six holes of golf, eighteen in the morning and eighteen in the afternoon, to be played under the most excruciating pressure. The murderous par 70 course had already taken its toll of many of the finest golfers in the 165-man field, including Demaret, Snead and Cary Middlecoff. "I'm putting like my doggone arms is broke," muttered Snead as he walked off the course after one particularly upsetting round.

Nothing seemed to be upsetting Hogan. He played his first eighteen holes that day in 72; another such round would undoubtedly win the title for him. But it had been two years since he had played 36 holes in one day and the heat out there on the course was enough to melt legs that were younger and sounder than his. He started well enough but the thousands of fans who made up his gallery saw that he was wilting. Sixteen months was not time enough to repair the frightful damage. He went one over par on both the fifteenth and seventeenth holes. By then the word had reached him: Lloyd Mangrum and George Fazio had each finished with a final total of 287. Ben needed a par four on the last hole to tie the two leaders and join them in a play-off on Sunday.

Hogan bowed his neck for a tremendous effort. He drove down the middle of the fairway, a good drive which put him in a favorable position on this dangerous 458-yard hole. His next shot went on the green, and then he was in the cup in two putts for his par four. There would be a play-off on Sunday and Ben Hogan would be in it.

He trudged painfully back to the clubhouse. Mangrum, winner of the 1946 Open, grinned at him. "See you tomorrow, Ben," he said.

Hogan let himself down into a chair. Then he settled back and a faint smile crossed his sweat-streaked face. "Yep, see you tomorrow."

"Tomorrow" was another hot day. Hogan was convinced that he could win the play-off by carding a par. Fazio was not a first-rate golfer and did not figure to offer him the competition he could expect from Mangrum. Lloyd was a gambler, and when his shots were falling right he was as good as anybody. Refreshed by a good night's sleep, the swelling in his legs down again, Hogan was bolstered by the confidence that is part of the make-up of every great champion. At the end of nine holes Hogan and Mangrum were tied with 36 each, while Fazio clung doggedly on with 37.

Now they were on the last nine holes. Hogan took a stroke lead over Mangrum on the tenth, but Lloyd got it back on the eleventh. Then Ben moved ahead again. Fazio finally dropped out of serious contention on the fourteenth and, after fifteen holes, Ben still had his one-stroke lead. And then came an incredible break. On the sixteenth, Mangrum lifted his ball to blow an insect from it. This was a stupendous blunder, a clear violation of the professional golfing rules against picking up a ball. He was penalized two strokes.

When Hogan learned of the incident his face, for the first time during the tournament, broke into a wide grin. Victory, he felt, was now assured, but victory in this tournament meant so much to him that he wanted it without the slightest taint. He wanted to win by more than the two penalty strokes. On the short seventeenth hole he drove his first shot to within fifty feet of the cup. He did not have a clear shot at it, though, for he had to putt over a rise. This was certainly a moment for caution. But Ben refused to "back in" to his title. The long putt, confidently stroked, rolled true to the cup and dropped in. As the spectators roared their approval, the usually stolid Hogan took off his cap, twirled it in his fingers and bowed low to acknowledge their tribute.

That was it. Ben shot a par four on the last hole to finish with a spectacular final round score of 69, four strokes ahead of Mangrum. The little man had come all the way back. As columnist Red Smith wrote the next day: "This was a spiritual victory, an absolute triumph of will."

And who won the *1951* Open? Why, Ben Hogan won that one, too.

Chapter 12 Derby Day

It is the same every year at the Kentucky Derby—the band playing, the magnificent but fragile horses moving around the paddock, people cluttering the infield and pushing their way up to the mutuel windows, those richly garbed and braceleted members of high society (who can never forget that racing is the "Sport of Kings") fluttering about the clubhouse and the unique air of excitement that seems to hover above horses and men. But Derby Day in 1951 was different for Conn Mc-Creary. He could remember back to a day in 1944 when he had been the center of attraction there in Louisville. And he could remember only a year ago when horsemen didn't even want to talk to him. Even now he wasn't on top of the world, but he was aboard a horse in the Derby and that was a privilege he never thought would be granted him again.

As he put on his silks in the jockeys' room that spring day, as jittery as a boy who was to ride in his first big stakes race, McCreary was left to himself. People still were not paying much attention to him. Yet there was one man who had confidence in him and that was all that mattered to Conn.

"With you up on him, Count Turf can win the Derby," Jack Amiel, the horse's owner, had said to McCreary some weeks before. Amiel still hadn't changed his mind, and his optimism imparted to Conn a measure of confidence, too.

The other jockeys, wrapped like party favors in their varicolored silks, bustled about the dressing room, filling the air with their chatter and complaints. Conn listened to the conversation around him and what he heard increased his confidence. Amiel had told him to ride the race as he thought best. Now a plan began to form in his mind. This day could be the turning point in his life.

A jockey can't run the race for a horse, but he can help to win it—or lose it. Those brave dwarfs who guide their mounts through narrow openings in the jam at the head of the stretch are, to many in the crowd, little more than gaudy ballast. Their humanity is granted only when they fail to bring a heavy favorite home in front—or when they fall under the sharp hoofs of the pack. Perhaps there are too many distractions at the track for the crowd to be aware of the riders' skill and fearlessness. A man holding a two-dollar bet on a 10-1 shot is not likely to be gripped by intimations of mortality, his or anyone else's.

The adulation which young Americans have lavished even on mediocre athletes in other sports has been withheld from jockeys. Apparently most day-dreaming boys are defeated by the paradox of wanting to "grow up" to be a jockey. Because a horse is at his best with the lightest possible load on his back, the qualifications for the riding profession are as strictly limited as they are for the position of a bearded lady in the circus; smallness is a requisite of the one, as shagginess is of the other. Jockeys, then, are small boys who didn't "grow up." It does not follow that the proportion of strength, intelligence, reflexes and courage found in jockeys is any less than that of their larger colleagues in sport. Danger, despair and frustration are common to men of all sizes and shapes, and so is the capacity to overcome them. We offer in evidence the story of Conn McCreary.

McCreary knew, when he was still very young, that he had stopped growing. He had the torso of a man, the legs of a small boy. In his late teens he stood four feet, eight inches tall and weighed about ninety pounds. He would, in the course of years, put on a few more pounds, perhaps, but those tiny legs (he measures only thirty-two inches from his waist to the ground) were an indication that he was as tall as he was ever going to be. Raised in St. Louis, he was as active as the other boys, developed powerful arms and shoulders and, until his stunted legs proved too much of a handicap, liked to take part in sprints on the running track.

Somehow Conn, the city boy, became crazy about horses. Perhaps he picked up his fondness for them as he watched the Westerns in his neighborhood movie house, perhaps he came to believe that it was more practical for him to do his racing on the back of a horse than on a cinder track where he had to take three or four steps for every one of the other fellow's. But Conn's passion for horses seemed to be one that would go unrequited. His father laughed off his request to buy him a pony. Conn could think of no other way in which a city boy would get the chance to be around horses as much as he would have liked. In desperation he sat down and wrote a letter to the only oracle he knew of—the "Advice to the Lovelorn" editor of a newspaper. She was of little help. She sent Conn the address of a local riding academy, whose docile old mounts were of no particular interest to a little fellow who had visions of becoming a hell-for-leather rider.

Finally Conn's desire to ride, coupled with a marked indifference to his studies, prompted him to leave school and set out to become a jockey. His father, aware that his fifteen-year-old son wanted to ride and not wishing to stand in his way, gave him bus fare and pocket money to carry him into the horse country. The only horse country that Conn had ever heard about was that around Lexington, Kentucky. Arriving there, he plodded along a dusty road past the big breeding farms, not quite knowing how to begin. Then a car, driven by an elderly gentleman with a weather-beaten face and imposing white whiskers, drew up alongside him and stopped.

"Can I give you a ride, son?" the man asked.

"Okay," Conn said, and climbed in.

"How far are you going?" the man asked.

Conn hesitated a moment. Then he spoke up. "I don't really know, sir," he admitted. "I want to be a jockey and I want to get a job working around horses at one of these farms."

"Have you ever worked with horses before?" the man asked.

Conn shook his head. "No," he admitted. "I'm from St. Louis. I really don't know much about them, but I want to learn."

And so the man, who was a horse trainer and whose name was Steve Judge, took McCreary to the Woodvale Farm and got him a job around the barns. It was there that the little guy first learned about horses. He hauled water and cleaned out the stalls and soon they let him exercise the horses in the mornings.

"The only thing I knew about riding horses," Conn was to say later, "was what I'd read in the papers or seen in the movies. I don't think any jock in the history of racing was as unprepared for his trade as I was. Most riders have been brought up around horses or their folks have been in the sport and riding comes natural to them. At the start I was climbing on and hoping for the best."

But he had a bigger handicap than ignorance. While jockeys are always small, few are as tiny as McCreary. Most of them are slender, but built along the lines of bigger men. McCreary's tiny legs were of no help to him when he was aboard a horse. Without the extra grip which his legs could have given him on a horse's sides, he was in constant danger of being tossed off. It was not until horsemen began to see that his powerful arms and shoulders were enough to control one-thousand-pound horses that they would trust him with valuable mounts in morning workouts. And, in 1939, Conn finally got his chance to ride in competition.

"I'll never forget the thrill of my first winner," he has said. "It was in the summer of 1939 at Arlington (Chicago) and I was on Florence M. She had never won a race, and neither had I—just a couple of maidens. But we came down the stretch in front and held on to win it."

It was to be over a year, though, before Conn would have the chance to prove he really could ride. In the meantime he was ignored by horsemen who still did not believe he would ever make a jockey. When he did get mounts they were invariably poor ones. Telling columnist Red Smith about those days, Conn has said:

"I remember that a man put me up in the second half of

the daily double once because his horse was in with ninety-six pounds and I was the only kid who could make the weight. The man told me he had three live daily double tickets on the horse and one of 'em was for me. During the parade they had the possibles up on the board, and my double price was just $9,976. Those three tickets the man had were the only ones sold on the combination. Well, I was in the lead in the back stretch and in the lead turning for home, and then something came past me and beat me about this far. Can you imagine what might of happened to me if I'd a win $9,976 then? I might never of rode."

After Conn had won his first race he moved on to New York, where he was on a horse in a $50,000 stake race. He had been given the horse, not for his skill, but for his lack of weight, which seemed to be his only asset at this stage of his career.

"Eddie Arcaro was in this race," Conn says, "and 'The Nose' was going to win this one, or else, because he didn't have the money then that he has now. Turning for home I was laying about fifth and the horse was moving around the leaders and a nice lane opened up on the rail and I slid through into the lead. Now here came Arcaro outside of me, and what a ride he was giving that horse! I looked over at him, and this was the greatest show I ever saw in my life. Down we came together, and I looked over at Eddie again and, honest, I can't describe it. I never saw such a ride as he was giving this horse. I stopped riding to watch, and he beat me a nose on the post. The jockey gets ten per cent of the winnings in a stakes race, so I had lost myself $5,000."

But now Conn was getting close to that kind of money. In the fall of 1940, when he was nineteen, he got a lift once more

from Steve Judge. The bewhiskered trainer gave him the kind
of mounts that a jockey must have to show what he can do, and
Conn quickly repaid Judge's faith in him. One of the horses
he rode that fall was Our Boots, the two-year-old champion
of 1940, and the young jockey's performances were so outstanding that he suddenly found he was in demand. He headed
for Florida that winter and, in the space of a couple of months,
made himself one of the most famous riders in America.

His rise in 1941 was as rapid as his fall was to be a few years
later. He was the leading jockey of the Florida season, topping
all other riders by winning forty-four races in the forty-six-day
meeting at Hialeah. A jockey may say that he has become a
star when the fans bet on him instead of on the horses. During
that first big meeting of his life the bettors rushed to the mutuel
windows at Hialeah to put their money on whatever horse he
was riding. The twenty-year-old rider appealed to them partly
because of his size, partly because of his performance and, perhaps most important of all, because of the manner in which he
won his races. Seventeen years later a horse named Silky Sullivan was to capture the public's imagination with whirlwind
finishes after apparently running a hopeless last through most
of his races. McCreary's technique was substantially the same.
He bided his time through most of the race, saving his horse
while letting the others run themselves out. Then he would
make his move at the top of the stretch and, with the crowd
roaring, he would come hurtling down to the finish line, over-
taking the front runners and leaving the spectators breathless
with excitement.

"He has a clock in his head," one old-time racing man said
of Conn. "If he makes his move an instant later than he does
he will not be able to catch up with the leaders; if he goes too

soon, his horse may run himself out before he reaches the wire. He has some kind of instinct that tells him when to go—and he cuts it as close as he can."

When the horses moved to Tropical Park that spring, Conn was the darling of the opening-day crowd. He was cheered as he came out aboard Fettacairn, the favorite, for the third race. He moved off with the others but, after only a few hundred feet along the backstretch, a cry went up from the crowd as the horses jammed and one of the riders went down.

"It's McCreary!" somebody shouted, and the cry was passed on through the crowd. "McCreary's down!"

A station wagon was sent out to where McCreary lay, but by the time it reached him he had climbed slowly to his feet. As he was helped into it the public-address announcer calmed the crowd with the words, "McCreary is practically unhurt and they are bringing him in now."

The crowd was waiting for him when he got back and, as he walked to the jockeys' house, his cap in his hand and his face smeared with the dirt of the backstretch, it sent up a warm cheer. In the dressing room there was a group of reporters waiting for him. McCreary had gone down in a spill and it was news. Whatever a star does is news.

And Conn, as one of the country's leading jockeys, rode in the Kentucky Derby that spring. He didn't win it, but everybody said that he would bring home a winner there, too, one day. That day came in 1944, when Conn won the Derby aboard Pensive. On top of that he rode Pensive to victory in the Preakness, then missed winning the Triple Crown by finishing second to Bounding Home in the Belmont. He was successful and exciting, and the men who owned the horses were as fond of him as the crowds were.

They say that the bigger they are the harder they fall. Well, no one ever fell so hard as little Conn. When, or how, his fall began no one can say for sure. But somewhere along the way, in the years after World War II, Conn lost his touch. The clock in his head was faulty now and those late rushes which once had carried him to victory were falling short in the stretch. Heavy favorites whom he knew he should bring home in front were coming home as also-rans. The instinct that had told him when to make his move now failed him. After Conn lost on a favorite at Belmont Park one day a racing writer shook his head and said:

"If they put Conn McCreary up on the horse that night instead of Paul Revere, we'd still be subjects of the King of England."

The fans stopped betting on McCreary's mounts and, even worse, the trainers looked elsewhere when they wanted a jockey in a big-stakes race. As one of them said in 1950, "McCreary? I don't even consider him a jockey any more. He's just so much dead weight on a horse's back. I don't know what's happened to him."

The dash and confidence which had once been his trademark had left him. His faith in himself shattered, he seemed to forget even the rudiments of riding. At Saratoga one summer he was thrown three times by his mounts in two weeks. George Cassidy, the starter there, recalls one of McCreary's most frustrating moments.

"They were in the gate and ready," Cassidy says, "and just as I pressed the button to send them off McCreary yelled:

" 'Not ready, sir! Not ready!'

"He yelled too late. What I hadn't been able to see was that he had one foot out of the irons. The gate came open and the

horses rushed out and there was Conn tumbling off and I can
still hear him hollering:

"'—— —— it! Here I go again!'"

His third fall at Saratoga was the most humiliating of all.
It happened as he came out of the starting gate, which was
placed, for that race, directly in front of the grandstand. He
slid awkwardly off the horse and fell in the dirt as the horse
galloped, riderless, away. He picked himself up and there was
rage in his eyes. An attendant handed him his cap, which had
fallen off, and another handed him his whip. The terrible frustration bubbled up within him and boiled over. He hurled the
cap to the ground and jumped up and down on it, then turned
away and beat himself viciously across his tiny legs with the
whip. The crowd in the packed grandstand, thinking it a
comical sight, laughed at him.

He was desperate now. He wanted to quit riding, but there
were his wife and four small children at home. All he knew was
horses, and even that knowledge had slipped through his fingers. There was one day when he thought he might pull out
of his slump. He had been given four mounts, and all of them
were good ones—for a change.

"I won with the first horse, and was disqualified. So I went
back and rode the next one and won again, but a couple of
minutes after the race I was notified that I'd been suspended
for ten days for an infraction in the first race. I was finishing
out the day, riding in the third race, when I got thrown coming out of the gate and my skull was fractured. Another rider
took my mount in the stakes race and won with it. It was a
great day for me. I got a disqualification, a suspension, a fractured skull and missed out on ten per cent of a big purse in the
stakes race."

Because he had nowhere else to turn, he kept riding despite failures and injuries. The mounts he got were few now, and they were in the smaller races and there were long stretches between them. In May, 1950, he went to Louisville hoping that he would be given a mount in the Kentucky Derby, but the trainers looked the other way when they saw him coming. There was no room for him at the hotel where once he had been catered to and pointed out as a famous man. Now he was just another little guy, down and out, hanging around during Derby week. He finally found a small room in a second-rate hotel. As he had not been invited to the parties where he was once a center of attraction, he trudged the streets alone.

The next spring, having been almost a year without work, Conn made the rounds of the barns. To keep in shape, he asked some of the trainers if he could exercise their horses in the mornings. A man who is willing to work for nothing has a good chance of finding employment. Conn worked the horses in the mornings and, after his long layoff, felt better again on the back of a horse. One of those he worked for then was Sol Rutchick, a man who trained horses for a number of small stables. Among the horses Rutchick trained was Count Turf, who had been sired by the great Count Fleet and was now owned by a New York restaurant man named Jack Amiel. Amiel knew little about horses, but it gave him a thrill to watch his colors in a big race, and he held out more hope than most horsemen did for Count Turf. Watching his horse work out in the mornings he got to know McCreary and liked the way he handled the horse. Count Turf was entered in the Wood Memorial that year, but he ran badly and finished up the track. His rider was McCreary.

"But I believed in Conn," Amiel said later. "He was a good

jockey once, so he's got to be a good jockey still. Things just broke wrong for him, that's all. I began to think that maybe things would begin to break for him after a while. Watching him and Count Turf work together helped me to think that way because he likes the horse and the horse likes him."

But no one else believed in either the horse or his rider. Rutchick advised Amiel that it would be a waste of money to send Count Turf to the Kentucky Derby. Amiel said nothing at the time. Then one day he met Conn around the barns.

"Are you going to send this horse to the Derby?" Conn asked him.

"Only if you ride him," Amiel said.

"I'm poison," the jockey said, shaking his head. "You know that."

"No," Amiel said, "I hear that, but I don't believe it. As far as I'm concerned you're a good jock. With you, Count Turf can win it. Without you, he don't go to Louisville."

When Amiel told Rutchick that Count Turf (and McCreary) were going to the Derby, the trainer lifted his eyebrows, shrugged and kept his own counsel. Later Rutchick said that other commitments would keep him in New York right up until Derby day. He told Amiel that he would send another trainer, George Sully, to look after the horse until he got there. Rutchick never made it to Louisville.

Since the decline of the big heavyweight championship fights the Kentucky Derby is probably the most dramatic single event in American sports. For a week before the Derby, people pour into Louisville and begin to put on what may be the most authentic mardi gras in the country. It is a period of parties and gambling, of funny stories and monstrous hangovers, of hope, excitement and despair. Two-dollar horseplayers mingle with princes, pickpockets and movie actors. All over the country people who have never been to a race track and who do not have the slightest interest in any other sports event turn their attention to Louisville and talk about the race for a week before it and a week after it.

Perhaps Conn McCreary, for whom the Derby was to mean so much, said it best of all while talking to a couple of newspapermen one day. "You know, it seems to me—" and here he hesitated for a moment, as if wondering to himself if he were exaggerating. But, having reassured himself, he went on. "It seems to me the Derby has come to be a kind of a religious thing in this country. Like for people that don't have any Confession."

And then it was Derby day. Racing men remember the 1951 Derby as "The Cavalry Charge," for the unwieldy number of twenty horses went to the post as the band played "My Old Kentucky Home." Battle Morn, with Eddie Arcaro up, was the favorite. Not one of the seventy-four writers and broadcasters who participated in a pre-race poll selected Count Turf for any of the three leading positions. At post time the horse was 15-1. It seemed that only Amiel and McCreary believed in the horse, and Conn, as he rode out onto the track, felt a pang that his wife was going to miss this moment. He had not been able to afford the price of a train ticket for her from Miami.

But uppermost in Conn's mind was his plan for the race. The night before he and Amiel had talked about the race and Amiel had pointed out that both Conn and Count Turf liked to hold back and come from behind with a rush. At the time this seemed to be their best chance. But, before going to bed, Amiel had told Conn that he had confidence in him and that he could switch the strategy if he saw anything that made him change his mind.

"I was glad he told me that," Conn said afterward. "When I got to the jocks' room before the race I tried to find out how the other jocks were going to ride. I didn't ask any questions, but I heard one boy say:

" 'I know my instructions are going to be to lay back and wait.'

"And then I heard a lot of the other boys say the same thing. So I figured that, if they were right, there would be only three or four horses going to the front and I would get right in behind them and not get caught back in the crowd. I knew the traffic would be heavy."

Conn got off well and moved in behind three or four horses who were running out in front. "I was so close to them," he said, "that a couple of times I looked down at my horse's front feet to be sure he wasn't stepping on anybody's heels." Along the backstretch Conn kept Count Turf tucked in behind the frontrunners and bided his time. When they came to the far turn, a horse moved up on the outside. Conn made his move. He pulled out to avoid being shut off by too many horses in front of him and in a moment he was battling Repetoire for the lead. As McCreary came alongside him the jockey on Repetoire swung over and bumped him.

"Hey! None of that!" Conn yelled, slamming back at the other. Repetoire gave ground and, going into the stretch, Count Turf took over the lead and won by four lengths.

It was a wonderful moment for McCreary. He was a hero again and there was a big smile on his face as he came bouncing into the jocks' room. The writers were there already, grouped around Arcaro while waiting for Conn to return from the winner's circle.

"To see all those reporters around you, you'd think you

had won the race," Conn said to Eddie as he squeezed past him.

"They just want to find out how I loused this one up," Eddie said, and then he grinned at McCreary, obviously happy for the little man.

"I feel so good," Conn said, "that I could even kiss you."

"You try it, you ugly-looking little ——, and I'll flatten you," Arcaro said. "Next to getting beat by you, the worst thing I can think of is being kissed by you."

And Conn could smile again. There were the questions by the reporters now, and the posing for pictures, and already there were requests coming in for Conn to handle other mounts. Later there was a check for $9,300, Conn's 10 per cent of Count Turf's winnings, and there was a gift from Amiel of a $1,000 bond to each of the four McCreary children. Finally there was the train ride with Amiel to New York, with writers and friends dropping into their compartment and, with each new visitor, Amiel pulling out the Derby's gold cup and showing it off.

"That's what we went out for," Amiel said, "the gold cup and the blanket of roses we have stashed away up in the refrigerator in the dining car. Anybody can make $93,000. But how many guys can win this gold cup?"

And Conn, looking at the cup like a small boy staring at— well, at a pony that he would prize above anything else if it were his own, said, "I wish they'd give a little cup for the jockey. I'd rather have that than the money—almost."

Conn was back on top. The people who run the Derby, knowing how much it meant to him, ordered a replica of the gold cup and gave it to him—a symbol of his remarkable comeback. As Conn had once said, "The Derby has come to be a kind of religious thing."

Chapter 13 Nothing Left but Heart

Dizzy Dean was the grandest figure in two World Series that were played only four years apart, yet the contrast between the Dean of 1934 and that of 1938 creates one of the most appealing of all baseball stories. Against the Tigers in 1934 he was in the full bloom of his overpowering pitching form and even more overpowering bravado; against the Yankees in 1938 he had lost all but his bravado. It is that first Series which Diz looks back on with nostalgia, and which will reflect to his credit in the record books. But for many of us the glory of 1934 will always lie in the shadow cast by his dogged courage in 1938.

Dean, who rose to greatness just as Babe Ruth went into his decline, took over the Babe's position as the game's most colorful player and biggest gate attraction. America likes its heroes to thump their chests and proclaim their invincibility—provided they can back up their boasts under fire. When John L. Sullivan thundered, "I can lick any man in the world!" and Ruth pointed to the distant bleachers before hitting a home run there, the crowd was on their side because they followed the dramatic gesture with the accomplished deed. Dean strutted in their footsteps.

"I'll tear them limb from limb," Diz said of the Tigers before the 1934 Series, and, when he had in truth dismantled them, the crowd swallowed its indignation and roared its approval. His bravado had embellished his performance. Of such stuff are our legends spun.

Like most legends, Dean came of hazy origins. The haziness was certainly partly authentic, and partly a result of Dizzy's own creative thinking. He was one of those who never let the facts stand in the way of a good story, and sometimes several good stories. Roy Stockton, who was Dean's closest friend among the sportswriters and who later helped to perpetuate the Dean legend in his book *The Gashouse Gang*, recalled an afternoon when he was present at several interviews given by the big pitcher to various newspapermen. There was at this time considerable mystery surrounding, among other vital points, the date and place of Dizzy's birth. Stockton maintained a determined but puzzled silence while Dean answered the questions put to him by the relays of writers. After the last group had left Stockton could no longer contain his curiosity.

"How could you do a thing like that?" he asked Diz.

"Like what?" Diz said blankly.

"Like giving each of those writers different answers to the same questions?"

"Why, Roy, you didn't expect me to give all of them fellers the same story, did you? Look here, now. They come from different papers and if they all went back with the same story their editors wouldn't like it and maybe they'd get real mad at them."

The authorized version now has it that Dean was born on January 16, 1911, at Lucas, Arkansas, but it is not known that he ever took an oath on this point. The facts of his childhood are equally undocumented. The son of a migratory worker in the South, he had a boyhood that did not afford him much stability. He later explained away part of the confusion with this tale:

"We was drivin' across the Southwest, me and Pa in one car, my uncle and my brother Paul in another car right behind us. We come to a railroad crossin' and there was a freight train headin' for it, too. Pa and me got across but Paul and my uncle didn't quite make it. It was a long train and, you know, we didn't see Paul and my uncle again for two years."

Dean's formal schooling was scanty, almost as scanty as the amount of truth to be found in the anecdotes he tells about his boyhood. "I didn't go to school but two years," he says. "If I'd gone another two years I'd have caught up to my Pa."

Diz once related to an audience the circumstances of his discovery by a big-league scout. It seems that he was throwing rocks at squirrels in the woods when an intrepid scout for the St. Louis Cardinals happened upon him.

"I was throwin' those stones with my *left* hand," Diz said, "and when that scout found out I was a right-hander he wanted to know how come I was usin' my left. I just told him the truth. I said that I threw so hard with my right hand that I squashed up them squirrels somethin' terrible, and they wasn't fit eatin' then."

The facts, as far as they can be determined, seem to be that Diz got tired of picking cotton and joined the Army in 1926. For those who have reminded him that, in 1926, he would have been only fifteen years old according to the "official" version of his birthday, Diz replies that he lied about his age to the recruiting officer. It was in the Army that he first made a reputation for himself as a pitcher. Learning that there was good money to be made by throwing a baseball past batters, he scraped up enough money to "buy" himself out of the Army, a practice that was common in those days. He entered organized baseball in 1930 and, late that season, he was in St. Louis, pitching and winning a game for the Cardinals.

He was back with the Cards in spring training the next spring. Everybody in camp agreed that they had never heard anybody quite like him. He seemed to have walked right out of a story by Ring Lardner—a big, brash kid who feared nobody, bragged of his ability and entertained his teammates with unlikely tales of his early youth. When the Cardinals played the world-champion Philadelphia Athletics in an exhibition game, manager Gabby Street decided that he would throw the young man to the wolves. He reasoned that a good pasting by the A's' sluggers would do more to silence Dean than a hundred reprimands. Street chose for him an inning in which the first three hitters for the A's were Mickey Cochrane, Jimmy Foxx and Al Simmons, one of baseball's most devastating group of sluggers.

"You go in next inning," he told Dean.

Diz took his warm-up pitches, then went to the mound, and struck out the three Philadelphia hitters.

"Nothin' but bush leaguers," he hollered to Street as he strutted off the mound.

But Street, having the veteran pitching staff which would carry the Cardinals to the world championship that year, decided Diz could use another season of experience in the minor leagues and shipped him to Houston. It has also been suggested that Street had seen and heard enough of the young man's escapades during spring training and was not anxious to have him in his hair all year. It seemed that everybody was to love Dizzy except his managers.

But they couldn't keep him off the team in 1932. By this time everybody was talking about the right-handed "Okie" with the big fast ball and the loud mouth. He led the National League in strike-outs and won eighteen games in his rookie season, then came back in 1933 to keep his strike-out title and win twenty games. On July 30 of that year he established the modern National League record by striking out seventeen Chicago batters.

"Heck," he said afterward in disgust, "if anybody told me I was settin' a record I'd of got me some more strike-outs."

Dean was attracting attention to himself in a variety of ways. There was a game against the Giants in which he bunted for a "home run." As there was a runner on first base when he came to bat, the Giants pulled their infield in, looking for a bunt. Diz, bunting it hard, blooped it over the head of the charging third baseman. The left fielder rushed in to pick up the ball and, as he saw Diz rounding first and heading for second, he threw there to head him off. The ball sailed over the second baseman's head into the right-field corner and Dean galloped home. It was not a "home run" officially; it was scored as a double and a two-base error. But it was another in a long line of incidents which were keeping his name in the newspapers. And Diz never objected to seeing his name in print.

He was treading on some toes, too, although it was difficult to hold a grudge against him for long. George Barr, an umpire, called a close decision against Diz one afternoon and the enraged pitcher rushed up to him.

"You mean to say that ball wasn't a strike?" Dean shrieked at the umpire.

Barr shook his head, then turned and walked away.

"Mr. Barr, ain't you even goin' to answer my question?" Dizzy called after him.

"I did answer your question, young man," Barr said. "I shook my head."

"No, you didn't. If you had I'd have heard somethin' rattle."

It was in 1934 that Diz became the brightest star in baseball and he dragged his brother, Paul, into the spotlight with him. Paul, of course, had a great deal of ability, too, and complemented his big brother perfectly. Diz, who knew how to blow his own horn, was even more extravagant in praise of his brother. Diz let everybody know that he was magnificent at everything he ever tried, but that his brother was just a little bit better. While Diz admitted he could throw hard, he claimed his brother could throw even harder; while he admitted that he could pick astonishing quantities of cotton in a day, he boasted that Paul could pick even more. Paul kept his mouth shut, let Diz do the talking for him and, for a couple of years, pitched very well indeed. Joining the Cardinals in 1934, he helped his big brother bring a pennant to St. Louis.

There were, however, a number of harrowing crises along the way. Frank Frisch, an aggressive, temperamental product of the John McGraw school of managing, had taken over the leadership of the Cardinals by this time and he demanded that his players think of nothing but victory. The Dean boys were to sprinkle his head with gray hairs before the season was over.

The basis for Dizzy's complaints was that he and his brother were being paid "coolie" wages. Their salaries for that year totaled only $10,500, Diz getting $7,500 and Paul, a rookie, only $3,000. Diz first claimed that his contract with the Cardinals was invalid. Talked into rejoining the team, he went on strike because he wanted his brother to get more money. While Diz refused to work, Paul went on pitching, never saying a word, and the "strike" was finally settled when Paul was granted a modest raise.

The disturbing Dean influence even touched rival managers. Bill Terry, the manager of the Giants, was holding a meeting with his team in the clubhouse one afternoon when the door opened and Dizzy walked in.

"What are you doing in here?" Terry asked, glaring at Dean.

"Oh, the Cardinals are holding a meeting in their clubhouse but none of them know what they're talkin' about so I thought I'd come over and visit you all."

"You can't come in here," Terry told him. "We're having a meeting of our own and we're talking about the weaknesses of the different hitters on your club."

Diz waved his hand and took a seat on a trunk. "That's okay with me. Go right ahead. I know all their weaknesses anyway, so you won't be tellin' me nothin'."

There was another day when he walked into the clubhouse of the Dodgers while they were holding a meeting. Manager Casey Stengel, whose experience with the group of clowns that played under him in Brooklyn prevented him from feeling surprise at any eccentricity among ballplayers, went right on talking. Taking each Cardinal batter in turn, he gave his players advice on how to pitch to them. When Casey had finished he turned to Dean and asked, "Was I right about how to pitch to you fellows?"

"Yep," Diz said. "And now, I'll tell you how I'm going to pitch against you guys today."

He singled out each Brooklyn hitter, reminded him what his weakness was and then went on to tell him exactly how he would pitch to him that afternoon. Finally he picked up his glove, strutted out of the clubhouse and shut out the Dodgers on three hits.

The Giants had moved off in front in the National League race and a runaway was prevented only by the Dean boys, "me and Paul," who beat them almost every time they faced them. Paul, quietly eccentric himself, had by this time earned the nickname "Daffy." Dizzy was the best pitcher in baseball now, and Daffy was among the best. Between them they were keeping the Cardinals in the pennant race. And then, on August 14, they ignited the biggest explosion of the season.

The Cardinals, like most ball clubs, picked up extra money on an off day by scheduling an exhibition game. As the Cards had agreed to stop in Detroit for a game on the way to St. Louis, all of the players were told to report for an early train. Dizzy and Daffy, deciding that they needed a brief rest, failed to go to Detroit. When they walked into the Cardinals' clubhouse the next day they were cornered by manager Frisch.

"You're fined $100 for not showing up in Detroit," Frisch said to Dizzy. "And your brother's fined $50."

Dizzy was outraged. He stormed through the clubhouse, swearing at Frisch and vowing he would never pay the fine and, what was more, he would see that Daffy didn't pay his fine, either. Then, while the team looked on in astonishment,

Dizzy picked up his uniform and tore it into shreds. "That's what I think of the Cardinals!" he roared. "I'm through with them!"

Dizzy and Daffy left the ball park, and Diz announced that, unless the fine was canceled, they would go fishing in Florida. "This is a dirty deal to give a fella who's tryin' to pitch the Cardinals to the pennant," he fumed. But the Cardinals replied that the fine was not going to be rescinded and, moreover, that they were billing Dean $36 for the uniform he had destroyed.

The Deans, like Achilles, remained sulking in their tents for a couple of days, but by the time it was their turn to pitch again they rejoined the team and paid their fines. Dizzy even reimbursed the Cardinals for the uniform, but it was a bitter pill for him to swallow. "They could have mended it," he grumbled.

The Deans were back in stride now and they took command of the race. Diz even had a good word to say for Frisch. "He's the greatest manager baseball's ever seen," he told a writer. "He's the only man who could keep a team in a pennant fight with a two-man pitchin' staff."

Diz was very nearly right about the Cardinals having a two-man pitching staff. Seven and a half games behind the Giants when they started their final eastern trip of the season, the Cardinals began to close the gap. It was the Deans who closed it for them. Meeting the Giants in an important series at the Polo Grounds, Daffy won the opening game by outpitching Fred Fitzsimmons in twelve innings, 2-0. Then, in a doubleheader two days later, Diz beat the Giants, 5-3, in the first game, and Daffy came back to win the second, 3-1. A few days later the Cardinals went to Brooklyn for a doubleheader. Diz pitched the first game, holding the Dodgers without a hit until the eighth inning when Ralph Boyle beat out an infield roller. Relaxing in the ninth, Diz gave up two more singles but held on to his shutout and won, 13-0. In the second game Daffy pitched a no-hitter. Diz was proud of his kid brother, but he had one complaint.

"I wished I'd known you was goin' to pitch a no-hitter," he said to Paul. "Then I'd have bore down and got *me* one, too."

The Cardinals overtook the Giants at the end of the season and won the pennant. Dizzy had been credited with thirty of their ninety-five victories, Daffy with nineteen. Then the elder Dean strutted into the World Series against the Tigers and provided the sportswriters with most of their copy. The day before the Series opened Diz appeared at the ball park in Detroit while the Tigers were at batting practice. The field was cluttered with writers, photographers and baseball men. After watching the Detroit players take their cuts for a few minutes, Dean suddenly peeled off his hat and coat, rolled up his sleeves and picked up a bat.

"Let a man hit that *kin* hit!" he yelled and, brushing aside an astonished batter, stepped to the plate and began to bang away at the batting-practice pitches. The photographers took all the pictures they could get and the writers had their stories for the day.

The next day's game was Dean's, too. Behind solid batting support he beat the powerful Tigers, 8-3. The game had been broken open in the sixth inning when the Cardinals clubbed Detroit's ace relief pitcher, Fred Marberry, for four runs. Diz was the center of attraction as he sat laughing and talking and boasting in the clubhouse afterward.

"Did you see that fella Marberry?" Diz howled over the din around him, "The way he come in there and drawed back and throwed his leg up in the air—he reminded me of somethin' that just come out of a fresh egg!"

The Cardinals lost the second game, but Daffy smothered the Tigers in the third, 4-1. Diz, fidgeting on the bench during the fourth game as the Cardinals trailed, came to life when they rallied in the fourth inning. When Virgil Davis, a slow-moving catcher, came up as a pinch hitter and singled, Diz could no longer remain out of the game. He had to help somehow. He leaped to his feet and, before anybody could stop him, inserted himself into the game as a pinch runner for Davis. Manager Frisch, startled, neglected to call him back. A moment later the Cardinals' hopes for victory in the Series came tumbling about their ears. Trying to complete a double play, Detroit shortstop Billy Rogell stepped on second to force the on-rushing Dean, then fired toward first base. But Diz could not get his head out of the way. The ball struck him flush in the forehead and knocked him unconscious. The Great Man was hauled off the field on a stretcher and it seemed that the Cardinals had lost their star.

They did not count on the irrepressible Diz. "Just as long as I didn't get hit on the arm I'm okay," he said from his hospital bed. "They took pictures of my head, and the X rays showed nothin'."

The next day he was back in uniform and pitching for the Cards. Only a fine performance by Tommy Bridges kept him from winning, and he was the losing pitcher in a 3-1 game. The Cardinals, down three games to two, had their backs to the wall, but Frisch still had the Dean boys on his side. Daffy beat the Tigers, 4-3, in the sixth game and Dizzy, behind a barrage of St. Louis hits, throttled them in the deciding game, 13-0. In the ninth inning of that game Dean began to torment the Tigers from the mound, throwing up the pitches they liked best to hit and grinning in childish delight. Frisch rushed over to Diz and threatened to take him out of the game.

"Imagine that!" Diz exclaimed later. "The greatest pitcher in baseball has a thirteen-run lead in the ninth inning and the manager is goin' to take him out. Why, when I looked around and saw he had four pitchers warmin' up in the bull pen I thought he was gettin' ready for the 1935 season. But old Frankie shouldn't have fretted."

There were two more great seasons ahead of Diz. He stuck his chest out and strutted around the league, beating the other teams, entertaining the writers and bringing fans to the ball parks wherever he pitched. His name was never out of the newspapers. In the winter, when baseball traditionally yields the headlines to other sports, Diz was still there, squabbling with the Cardinals' owners about his salary or making sarcastic comments about other players and teams. Even Daffy made the headlines one winter.

"I think all the other players on this club ought to volunteer to take a cut," Daffy said, "so's Diz can get the salary he wants."

There is no record of the other players' seconding the motion of the younger Dean. But, sooner or later, the Cardinals and Dean always came to terms and the Cardinals invariably reported that Diz was receiving a lot of money. Diz just as invariably responded, "I'm worth it."

If Dizzy's years of greatness were to be brief, Daffy's were even briefer. When Daffy won nineteen games again in 1935 (his big brother won twenty-eight), he had posted his last successful record. Arm trouble soon drove him out of the majors. Dizzy was still going strong, however, and won 24 games in

1936, then got off to a fine start in 1937. He was chosen, as usual, for the National League All-Star team and it was in the All-Star Game at Washington that disaster finally caught up with him. A line drive from the bat of Earl Averill smashed into his foot. Taken to the hospital, he was found to have suffered a broken toe. He attempted to pitch again before the toe had healed, injured his arm in affecting an unnatural motion, and the great fast ball which had terrorized the league disappeared forever.

Diz was of little use to the Cardinals for the remainder of that season. As St. Louis officials watched him try to get in shape during the next spring they became convinced that he would never regain his original speed. The Chicago Cubs, gambling for a pennant in 1938, were willing to go high for him. They bought him from the Cardinals for $270,000 in cash and players.

"The Cubs will win the pennant," Dizzy announced, and headed for Chicago.

For a while it appeared that the Cubs would get no return on their investment. Dean had nothing left. Even when he threw his soft stuff his arm hurt him and he spent more time in doctors' offices than on the pitching mound. He kicked up a mild rumpus in July when he announced that, because he had been overworked in St. Louis and his arm was permanently damaged, he was going to sue the Cardinals for $250,000. His statement made the headlines, as almost everything he said did, but the storm soon subsided and Dizzy went back to pitching. It was characteristic of him that, with the Cubs battling for the pennant in September, Dean began to show signs of life once more. The fast ball was gone but, proving that he was smarter than many people had given him credit for being, he

called on all of the pitching tricks he had learned, but never
needed, during his brighter days. The fans flocked to the park
to see him pitch and he became as big a favorite in Chicago
as he had been in St. Louis. In a poll conducted by the Advertising Club there to determine Chicago's outstanding attraction, Diz finished in a tie for first prize with the zoo's
giant panda. Diz graciously reported that he was honored.

His arm trouble had not robbed him of his boundless self-
confidence. He was enjoying himself immensely through the
Cubs' drive, especially as his old teammates in St. Louis had
dropped out of the race. He had showed them that they
couldn't get along without old Diz. The Pittsburgh Pirates
were the Cubs' principal contenders for the pennant and,
when they invaded Wrigley Field at the end of September for
the showdown battle, Chicago was in a frenzy. The gathering
war clouds in Europe, the saber rattling of Hitler, the desperate
efforts of Western European statesmen to soothe the German
dictator—all were pushed out of the headlines. The Cubs were
on the threshold of a pennant, and their fate was in the hands
of a pitcher who had been almost helpless for over a year. Dean
pitched the big game.

He gave it everything he had, standing off the Pirates for
eight innings, preserving the Cubs' narrow 2-0 margin and
earning an ovation as he strutted back to the dugout after
each inning. His arm finally gave out in the ninth inning, but
by then the Pirates had missed their chance. Bill Lee came in
to relieve Diz and retired the final batter. The Cubs won the
game, 2-1, and the pennant was theirs.

The joy of the Cubs in victory was tempered by the knowledge that they had to face the Yankees in the World Series.
This was the Yankee team many baseball men have considered

the finest ever put together. Lou Gehrig . . . Joe DiMaggio . . .
Bill Dickey . . . Joe Gordon . . . Tommy Henrich . . . Red
Rolfe . . . Frankie Crosetti . . . These were the players who
had just completed their third straight runaway in the American League and were heading for their third straight easy
victory in the World Series. When the Yankees beat Lee, the
Cubs' ace pitcher, in the opening game, it was obvious that they
were on their way to another world championship.

In an attempt to keep the Series from turning into a rout
the Cubs gave Dean the pitching assignment in the second
game. Such an assignment would have been a formidable challenge to Dean even in his prime; now, with nothing left but
his confidence and his knowledge of the hitters, he had only
the slimmest chance against the Yankees. A crowd of 42,000
people, drawn by the drama that was to be unfolded on the
afternoon of October 6, jammed Wrigley Field and hoped
for the impossible.

Diz, throwing his "nothing ball," got by the first inning but
was hit by misfortune in the second. With two Yankee runners on base, shortstop Billy Jurges collided with third baseman Stan Hack as he went after a slow roller hit by Joe
Gordon. The ball trickled past them into left field and the
two runners came home to put New York ahead, 2-1. But
Dean hung on, battling the Yankees inning after inning,
strutting on and off the field, just as he had done four years before with the Cardinals, and looking every inch the master
of the situation. The Cubs scored twice in the third and led,
3-2. Now it was up to Diz.

For a while it looked as if he would get away with it. His
slow pitches frustrated the Yankees' sluggers, keeping them off
balance and forcing them to go for the pitch that Diz wanted

them to hit. He was a man holding off lions with a fly swatter. He still clung to his one-run lead as the Yankees came to bat in the eighth inning. He got the first two batters, then walked pinch hitter Myril Hoag. The next batter was Crosetti, the weakest hitter in the Yankee line-up. Diz pitched and Crosetti, timing the pitch perfectly, walloped it over the left-field wall for a home run.

The blow was greeted by almost complete silence. The crowd knew that it was the end of Dean's magnificent effort. Dizzy, stunned for a moment as he watched the ball disappear over the wall, quickly recovered his bravado. As Crosetti trotted around second base Diz came off the mound, almost running toward the Yankee shortstop, and screamed, "You wouldn't have hit one like that off me two years ago, you little——!"

And Crosetti, turning third now, looked over at Dean and grinned. "I know it, Diz," he called.

It was, of course, the end for Dean. It didn't matter that DiMaggio hit another home run against him in the ninth inning. The game had already been lost. The Series, too, had been lost and the Cubs, with all the fight gone from them now, fell weakly before the Yankees in four straight games.

It had been an easy Series for the Yankees, but they remembered Dean. Winning or losing, Diz left his mark on his opponents. He departed from the big leagues soon afterward. He could not remain there on heart alone, but no one who saw it will ever forget him on that afternoon when he carried little but his heart into the battle against the Yankees. The records will show that he was the losing pitcher; but when he strutted off the field he took with him his most memorable triumph.

Chapter 14 Campy's Ordeal

"I was driving towards home. I was almost there," Roy Campanella said as he recalled those terrifying moments in the early morning of January 28, 1958. "When I got to this sharp turn in the road the car must have hit a little patch of ice. It skidded, hit a pole and turned over. I guess I never really blacked out because the first thing I thought about was the car catching fire. I was pinned in the front seat and I tried to reach the ignition key. But I couldn't move my arm."

The wonderful world that Campy had constructed for himself had just dissolved in the sickening crash of the rented convertible he was driving. The twisting road in suburban Glen Cove, Long Island, was shrouded in chilly darkness. As he lay helpless in the wreckage there was only an echo of the sound of grinding metal to pierce the frightening silence that descends for a moment after an accident.

The neighborhood came to life slowly. A light went on here and there in the nearby houses. There was the faraway murmur of excited and curious voices. A doctor, summoned by someone who had heard the crash, finally arrived and peered into the overturned car. When a flashlight lit up the injured man's face a bystander recognized him.

"It's Campy!" the man exclaimed. And the word was passed around. "It's Campy!" Everybody in the neighborhood knew by sight the great ballplayer who had moved into their midst three years before.

Now an ambulance was on the scene and Campy was lifted carefully out of the wreck and rushed to Glen Cove's Community Hospital. From there the word went out to the nation that the Dodgers' great catcher lay paralyzed and near death. It is seldom that the public has reacted with such genuine sadness to the news of a prominent man's tragedy. Calls and messages flooded the hospital. Reporters waited in the corridors for more news as surgeons performed on Campy a four and a half hour operation to correct the damage done to his vertebrae and relieve the pressure on his spinal cord.

After the operation his wife, Ruthe, sat waiting for hours at his bedside. Only when the doctors had assured her that he seemed, for the moment, at least, out of danger and and that she could not be of any more help, did she prepare to leave. As she picked up her coat she looked down at the still figure in the bed and was startled to see him looking up at her.

"Be careful driving home," he whispered.

Ruthe smiled through her tears as she looked down at her husband. "I'll be back in a little while," she said.

"I'll be here," Campy whispered. "I ain't going anywhere."

As a ballplayer, Roy Campanella had attracted one of the

game's largest personal followings; his homey philosophy, his delightful way with children, his roly-poly figure and his dramatic home runs made him a favorite even with those who normally cared little for baseball. As a human being battling courageously and doggedly to overcome his paralyzing injuries, he was an invaluable inspiration to untold thousands of handicapped people all over the country. It was easier to stop feeling sorry for oneself after contemplating Campy's ordeal.

No one who knows him could have been surprised by his tenacious struggle to regain his health. Campy has been battling obstacles all his life. He overcame what must have seemed to him the insurmountable barrier of baseball's color line and did it without suffering the psychological scars with which many of his fellow Negroes came out of the struggle. He made astonishing comebacks after serious injuries in baseball and never lost the good humor for which he had become famous. His teammates, the men who knew him best, called him "The Good Humor Man."

He delivered his corny jokes and homey philosophy in a high-pitched voice that delighted his listeners. His humor was apt to break out at any time. During one important game Roy was catching his roommate, big Don Newcombe. He signaled for a fast ball but, for some reason, Newk threw a slow curve instead. Campy ambled out to the mound, scowled at Newk and asked in his high voice:

"Hey, Roomie, how come you throw me the local when I called for the express?"

His enthusiastic chirps and unusual expressions could lift the tension during the tightest moments on a ball field. "You can't be a dead pants out there," he would say. "You gotta liven things up."

He chattered even to the opposing players who came to bat when he was catching. Sometimes he would make fun of them, sometimes he would try to distract them from the business at hand with comments about whatever subject happened to pop into his mind. When Willie Mays, a naïve youngster, first came to the Giants, Campy plagued him with chatter. Willie, knowing of Roy's immense reputation as a big-league star, respectfully answered all of his questions with a "Yes, Mr. Campanella," or a "No, Mr. Campanella." Meanwhile, Willie began to discover that he was spending so much of his time answering Roy's questions that he seldom got a hit against the Dodgers. There came a day when Campy was particularly talkative. Willie could stand it no longer. Finally he turned around, stamped his foot in frustration and screeched:

"See here, Campy! You let me be!"

Campy's teammates looked on his chatter in a different light. The players, along with reporters and other visitors to the Dodgers' dugout, would gather around the rotund catcher as he told yarns about the days when he played in the Negro leagues. Stretching a point here and there and adding his own choice expressions he would recall the time that he caught four games in one day and the season that he caught a whopping total of 275 games. Or, sometimes, he would have his listeners commiserate with him over the days when he had to exist on the 50 cents a day which the team manager doled out to him as meal money.

One of his favorite tales was of a game he played in Venezuela's winter league. "Big Luke Easter was playing third base for the other team," Roy would say. "Man, he's a monster! I was on second base and the next batter hit a single. I scampered down to third and took my turn there but Luke was

standing in my way. I tore into him and knocked him flat
and then I kept right on going for home plate. Luke must have
bounced right up because all of a sudden I hear him chugging
along right behind me. I crossed the plate and just kept on
running. When I got to the dugout I hollered, 'Take care of
him, Newk,' and I didn't stop until I got to the clubhouse."

Roy could hold a large audience at an important banquet as
skillfully as he could the small groups in the Dodger dugout.
Asked to make a speech, he would get slowly to his feet and in
a few moments the audience would be chuckling or weeping,
depending upon the tone of Campy's message. His beaming
face exuded a kind of homey charm and the way his voice rose
to a high squeak when he became excited invariably charmed
his listeners. The roundness of his body disguised the hard
muscles that lay just beneath the surface and gave him the
appearance of a dusky, whiskerless Santa Claus. With the
unfailing instinct of a great actor he sprinkled his talks with the
appropriate pauses or the dramatic emphasis on certain points
that lifted them onto the level of real entertainment.

He was just as effective on television. In that faraway time
when Brooklyn had a baseball team, there was a television
program broadcast from Ebbets Field before each game. Conducted by Happy Felton, the program was called The Knot-
Hole Gang and three sandlot players appeared on it each day.
The boys were asked to pitch or field grounders and fly balls,
and the one judged the best was allowed to return to the show
on the following day and interview the Brooklyn player of
his choice. A large percentage of the boys asked for Campy.

"He always had a special way with kids on the program,"
Felton said recently. "He never talked down to them but when
they asked his advice about something he gave it to them

straight. I remember one day a boy asked him how he could correct his batting stance. Campy had the boy show him his present stance, then suggested he move his left foot back a little.

" 'How's that, son?' Roy asked him and the boy said it felt good. Then Campy said, 'See, your stance is corrected already. You got to feel good before you can hit good.' "

Campy always had the simple, direct approach to baseball because that was the way he learned the game in the Negro leagues. "I never heard of a slider or a sinker until I got in the Brooklyn organization," he once said. "We saw them in the colored leagues, sure, but what they call a slider here was just a curve that hardly broke and a sinker was a curve that only broke down. They didn't have no names for them in the colored leagues."

Like all good-natured men Campy was the object of his colleagues' humor, too. They poked fun at him about his weight, about the mustache he usually showed up with at spring training and about his age. They suspected that Roy, taking a leaf from Jack Benny's book, always gave himself the best of it when asked how old he was. Campy just as stoutly maintained that he was telling the Gospel truth.

The liquor store he owned in Harlem came in for its share of kidding, despite the fact that Roy was not much of a drinker himself. During batting practice one day the Dodger players looked up into the stands to see a fistfight in progress between a couple of fans.

"Hey, Campy," Gil Hodges shouted, "it looks like a couple of your customers are going at it up there."

"No, sir," Campy piped, shaking his head vigorously. "I don't sell any of that fighting liquor. I just sell *happy* liquor."

The success that Roy was enjoying until the tragic day of his accident had not been easy for him to attain. He was born in Philadelphia of an Italian father and a Negro mother. The date, as far as diligent investigation can determine, was November 19, 1921. He was never quite able to convince his teammates that this was so and they continued to believe that Campy was almost as old as Abner Doubleday. One of the reasons for this belief was that he apparently left school at the age of fifteen and immediately began playing with a local Negro team. By the time he reached the Dodgers he had accumulated so many years of experience in the Negro leagues that his new teammates assumed he was an old man.

As a boy Roy had told people that he would play in the major leagues when he grew up. He was puzzled at the bitter laughter which this remark always occasioned. It was not until he was older that he discovered that, as matters stood, the majors were forever out of his reach. A "gentleman's agreement" among baseball people barred Negroes from organized ball. Even this discovery could not stop him. He continued to play the game with all of his customary enthusiasm.

Then, when World War II had ended, a whole new horizon was opened for Campanella and the other Negro stars. Branch Rickey, the president of the Dodgers, signed Jackie Robinson to be the majors' first colored player. Campy's years of playing ball under bad lights in the tank towns had finally paid off. Signed by the Dodgers, too, he moved up quickly through their farm system. While playing at St. Paul during the summer of 1948, he was summoned to Brooklyn. This was his chance. He arrived in Brooklyn on July 1, just in time for a night game against the New York Giants. When he walked into the

Dodgers' clubhouse Leo Durocher, who then managed the team, turned to the clubhouse man and said:

"Give him a uniform."

The clubhouse man, John Griffin, picked out a uniform he thought might fit Roy and tossed it to him. "Try this one," he said.

Roy put it on. "It fits okay," he said.

He wasted no time in winning over the Brooklyn fans. Durocher put him in the starting line-up and, in his first time at bat, Roy doubled high off the right field wall. He got two more singles that night and was retired only once—on a long fly to the left fielder. Afterward he went up to Griffin in the clubhouse and grinned.

"Never mind hunting up a new uniform for me," he said. "This 39 must be my lucky number."

He wore that number throughout his career with the Dodgers. His performance that first night had made Campy and his number a big favorite at Ebbets Field and he kept right on winning ball games and friends. He got two singles, a triple and a base on balls the next afternoon against the Giants, then smashed a single and two tremendous home runs in the final game of the series. In this three-game series, the first of his big-league career, Campanella had collected nine hits and a base on balls in thirteen times at bat. He was on his way.

It was not only the players and reporters who were able to sense Campy's exuberance. His boundless good nature and his enthusiasm for baseball were transmitted to the fans in the grandstand, too. "You know," Campy once said, "you got to have a lot of little boy in you to be a ballplayer." He played the game with a little boy's delight and a man's skill.

If it were not for the injuries which constantly plagued

him Campanella almost surely would have gone down as the best catcher baseball has ever had. By 1951 he was at the peak of his career. Tris Speaker, who was one of the game's greatest stars during the first quarter of this century, watched Campy play a few times and later said of him:

"Of all the men playing baseball today the one they will talk about the most twenty or thirty years from now will be Campanella."

He was a skillful catcher, a shrewd student of the opposing hitters and a master psychologist with his own pitchers.

"Campy knows everything," Johnny Podres, then a young lefthander with the Dodgers, said in a tone of voice that bordered on hero worship.

"I got to," was Campy's reply. "That's a catcher's job. Some of you fellows won't move off the mound until I call a play at first base for you. Some of you fellows got to keep being reminded of a runner at first base who looks like he wants to steal."

Nineteen fifty-one was a strange year. A hot water heater blew up in Campanella's face before the season opened, searing his eyes and nearly blinding him. During spring training he suffered a fractured thumb. During the season he was hurt several times, most seriously when he was hit in the head by a pitch thrown by Turk Lown of the Cubs. The Dodgers missed him sorely whenever he was forced out of the line-up. But, so devastating was his slugging when he was in the game that, at the season's end, he was voted the Most Valuable Player in the National League.

But Campanella could not put two good seasons together. Injuries hobbled him badly in 1952 and his slugging fell off. He never lost confidence in himself, though, and he came swinging back in 1953 to have the greatest year any catcher has ever had. He batted .312, led the league with 142 runs batted in and hit 41 home runs. His home-run, runs-batted-in and putout totals all were new major league records for a catcher, and he won his second Most Valuable Player Award. His third such award was given him in 1955, following an injury-riddled 1954 season. Then, bad luck, which included a severed nerve in his left hand, hampered him for the rest of his career.

Campy was one of the few players whose enthusiasm for playing baseball did not diminish as he grew older. "I never want to quit playing ball," he once said. "They'll have to cut this uniform off me to get me out of it." (That remark has a particularly ironic ring to it now.) The little boy in Campy never completely disappeared. He poured all of his bubbling love of life into baseball, because the game had been his life for so many years.

Off the field he indulged himself in many ways, but his hobbies were always those in which his family could participate. He moved his wife and six children into a luxurious ten-room house in Glen Cove, Long Island, and started building his collection of electric trains up to its peak of 68 locomotives and 443 cars. A friend of his once commented on them:

"Roy, your kids sure must love electric trains."

"Kids?" Roy piped. "They're *my* electrc trains!"

He bought a forty-one-foot twin-screw cruiser for his family and named it *Princess*, after his youngest daughter. And for years he owned a large collection of tropical fish. "The kids and me, we'd just sit there by the hour, watching them fish," he recalled not long ago. "It kept us together, the kids and me."

When Edward R. Murrow began his television program, *Person to Person*, he chose the Campanellas to appear on the opening show. Campy, with his gift for chatter and cracker-barrel humor, was an ideal guest, and his attractive wife, the children and his many hobbies all helped to make the telecast an immensely compelling one.

And then Campy's world came tumbling down around him on that January morning. He could never again play the game he loved. The comfort and security he had provided for his family were threatened by the terrific medical expenses and the destruction of his means of earning a living. He faced life as a hopeless cripple. Campy's friends feared that even his good humor and resolution must crack under the blow that fate had given him.

There were those, however, who remembered Campy's reactions to the toughest situations on a ball field. When the Dodgers were driving for the pennant in 1953 manager Charley Dressen used to promise free beer to the players in the club-house after a winning game. In the late innings of those close games when the Dodgers needed a big hit and Campy came to bat with men on base, the players in the dugout used to send up a delighted cry:

"Ice up the beer, Charley! Here comes Campy!"

Now Campy was in a situation tougher than any he had ever faced on the field. He didn't quit now, either. Soon the reports of the close friends who had been admitted to see him in the hospital began to filter through to the public. Carl Erskine, one of Roy's old teammates, came out of the hospital room to say:

"He's the same old Campy. He's got the same round face and he's always smiling. Just talking to him there, I got the impression that he was more concerned about how bad the team has been going than about his own condition."

And Frank Slocum, an assistant to baseball commissioner Ford Frick, paid Roy an early visit. "Things were still touch and go with him," Slocum said later, "but he looked up at me and said, 'I'm scufflin', believe me.'

"Just before I left a nurse brought him some pills and a glass of cranberry juice. She had to hold the glass for him while he sipped the juice through one of those glass straws. He made such a face that I had to laugh.

" 'What's the matter?' I asked him. 'Don't tell me you don't like cranberry juice.'

"He muttered something. With the straw in his mouth I couldn't hear exactly what he said but it sounded suspiciously like, 'Cranberry juice stinks.'

" 'That could be,' I said, 'but I'll bet it tastes better than some of the stuff you sell in that liquor store of yours.'

"Well, Campy just spit out the straw and looked at me indignantly and said in that high voice of his, 'I couldn't move stuff as bad as this in my store.'

"Then he laughed, and I figured it was a good time to leave."

Laughter, too, can shed light on a great heart.

Chapter 15 **A Day in the Sun**

It began as a miserable day for Bobby Thomson. The Giants had been slaughtered, 11-0, the day before as the Dodgers had evened the 1951 play-off for the National League pennant at one game apiece. Now the Giants were playing as if they were going to throw the deciding game away, too. Thomson came to bat with Whitey Lockman on first base in the second inning and lined a hit to left field. Lockman went to second and stopped. Thomson, his head down, raced around first base and steamed into second with what he thought was a double. Then he stood gaping at his teammate as the Dodgers, delighted at the sight of two Giant runners standing on the same base (a feat for which they were supposed to hold the copyright), tagged Bobby out.

And then in the eighth inning, after Thomson's long fly in the seventh had driven in Monte Irvin with the run that tied the game at 1-1, the Dodgers threatened to blow the game wide open. Two hits and a wild pitch broke the tie. A hard-hit ball that Thomson, playing third base, couldn't come up with gave the Dodgers their third run. A moment later it was 4-1 as still another hit went through the star-crossed Thomson. And so it went until the bottom of the ninth inning when the Giants got their last chance against Brooklyn's big right-handed pitcher, Don Newcombe. The Giants' incredible drive apparently had petered out. They had given it a wonderful try, and nobody could have asked any more of them.

Still, it was tough to lose once they had gone this far. On August 13 they had trailed the league-leading Dodgers by 13½ games. There was no question but that the Dodgers' dominant position was authentic, for their team boasted Jackie Robinson, Duke Snider, Roy Campanella, Pee Wee Reese and the other great players who were to bring pennants to Brooklyn in four of the next five seasons.

Then, almost imperceptibly at first, the Giants began to move up on them. Some of the Dodger sluggers like Duke Snider and Gil Hodges fell into long batting slumps. The Dodger pitching staff, so impressive earlier in the season when it had had the support of murderous hitting, began to reveal itself as painfully thin. At the same time everything began to break in favor of manager Leo Durocher and his Giants. When the two teams moved into September it became apparent that the Giants' drive was not an illusion. The tension, which had been building slowly, now became almost unbearable for the teams and their followers. "The Creeping Terror," as sportswriter Bill Corum called the Giants, was right on top of the Dodgers and it seemed a good bet that Brooklyn would crumble under the pressure before the final game.

The Giants, having wiped out the "insurmountable" lead, went into a tie for first place with the Dodgers during the last weekend of the season. The season closed on a Sunday and the Giants, playing the Boston Braves, won their game and then settled back to celebrate when they learned that the Dodgers were losing in Philadelphia. But now the Dodgers began to battle back. They tied up the game in the eighth inning and, in one of the most dramatic contests that anyone could remember, went on to win in fourteen innings on Jackie Robinson's home run. The season had ended in a tie, and a three-game play-off was needed to determine the league champion.

The Giants won the opening game on a home run by Bobby Thomson, 3-1, and then were buried during that nightmarish rout, 11-0. Now the big moment had been reached. Like the culmination of any good drama, it had come after a steady progression of perilous steps had carried the plot to its ultimate point. It could not be prolonged much further without risking the chance that the tension would dissolve in a puddle of absurdity. The crowd that jammed the Polo Grounds in New York on this memorable October 3 shouted encouragement to the Giants, but got ready to head for the nearest exit as soon as Newcombe should get the side out.

The inning started with singles by Al Dark and Don Mueller, and the crowd stirred. It settled back again when Monte Irvin popped out. Then Whitey Lockman brought the old park alive with a two-base hit, driving in Dark and sending Mueller to third. There was a dramatic delay now as Mueller, injured while sliding into third base, was carried from the field on a stretcher and the Dodgers replaced Newcombe with Ralph Branca.

When play was resumed Thomson was ready to bat against Branca. Durocher came down to talk to Bobby.

"What did Leo say to you?" a reporter asked Thomson later.

"He told me, 'Bobby, if you ever hit one, hit one now.'"

"And what did he say after it was all over?"

"He couldn't say anything. He was crying like a baby."

The Brooklyn pitcher, beaten by Thomson's homer in Ebbets Field only two days before, fired a fast ball over for a strike. He was pitching desperately now, for the tying runs were on base. He got his next pitch over the plate and Thomson, with the most famous single swing in baseball history, connected and drove it into the lower left-field stands for a home run.

That blow won the ball game and the pennant for the Giants. It should eventually cause a statue of Thomson to be erected in the game's Hall of Fame at Cooperstown, New York, too. Baseball feeds on its legends and even disinterested observers, looking back at the incident today, cannot but feel that there was more of the legendary than of the real about Thomson's blow. It was the yea-sayers' version of "Casey at the Bat."

Many players, of course, have fashioned more impressive careers for themselves than Thomson has, but none has made so sharp an impact with one stroke. This is one of the consolations of the athlete—that, with a single extraordinary performance he can gild a career which otherwise might be quickly forgotten. The fame of the very greatest athletes rests on their ability to play brilliantly over a long period of time. But sharing a place in the history of sports are the athletes who justified a lifetime of competition by that one act which lifted them into the company of the immortals. That they will be remembered chiefly for this one day of glory does not imply that they were lucky. Most were fine athletes in their own right, but below the top level. To some their big moment came early in their careers, to others it provided a climax. Talented and determined they always did the best they could and were ready to seize fame as it raced by them.

Among these are the athletes we shall remember more vividly for one losing battle than for all their many triumphs. What football fan will forget Kyle Rote? Kyle was a teammate of Doak Walker at Southern Methodist University. Immensely talented himself, he was nevertheless overshadowed by the magic name of Walker through most of his college career. In 1949, Walker's senior year (Rote was a junior), the Doaker remained in the headlines right up until the final game of the season. And then, when it became evident that his leg injury would keep him out of the line-up against Notre Dame, SMU's slim chances for victory disappeared. It had been hoped in Texas that the brilliant Walker might be able to keep the Mustangs in contention for a while, for anything less than their best would not be good enough against the Fighting Irish. This invincible postwar Notre Dame team was on its way to its fourth straight undefeated season. As it was, SMU was forced to field a makeshift lineup. Rote was moved over from wingback into Walker's tailback position. Seventy-five thousand people jammed the Cotton Bowl in Dallas that day; they kept their fingers crossed that they would see the semblance of a contest before the dikes broke and Notre Dame turned the game into a rout.

They saw a magnificent game. Although Notre Dame led, 13-0, at the end of the first half, the Mustangs had battled for every inch of ground and Rote's performance on offense and defense had been exceptional. His performance in the second half was miraculous. When the half opened, SMU smashed 71 yards in five plays to a touchdown. Rote made all but 17 of those yards and finally scored on an end run. Gambling now, the Mustangs tried a pass from deep in their own territory the next time they got the ball, but the Irish intercepted it and scored. As the teams entered the final quarter Notre Dame appeared to have a commanding edge, 20-7.

But Rote and the Mustangs were still in the game. On a spectacular play, he passed to Johnny Champion from his own 31-yard line and the little halfback carried the ball all the way to Notre Dame's one-foot line. Rote slammed over for a touchdown on the next play and the score was 20-14. A few moments later the Mustangs had the ball again and were driving toward the Irish goal for another score. Rote set up the touchdown by racing around end to the Notre Dame four, and then needed only two more rushes to get the ball into the end zone.

And now the score was 20-20 and the crowd was in an uproar. This undermanned SMU squad was threatening to upset what many experts thought was the finest college football squad ever assembled. But the Irish carried too many guns for SMU. Taking the next kickoff, they swept down the field for the touchdown which put them ahead, 27-20. Such a convincing demonstration of speed and power would ordinarily have taken the heart out of a club which had battled so resolutely to tie the game just seconds before. But Rote and his fired-up teammates were not yet through. As time ran out they stormed the Irish goal again, but the clock was against them. Kyle had gained 115 yards rushing, passed for 146 yards, averaged 48 yards a punt and scored three touchdowns. Only time

could beat a team like Southern Methodist and a player like
Kyle Rote.

One of the quickest ways in which a ballplayer can win
fame is to pitch a no-hitter. It is a superlative feat, one in which
the pitcher shows his absolute mastery over another team
during the course of a full game. Almost one hundred no-
hitters have been pitched since 1900, but two men stand out
among all the rest of the no-hit hurlers for the dramatic nature
of their accomplishments. One is Johnny Vander Meer, who
pitched two consecutive no-hit games, and the other is Don
Larsen, the only man ever to pitch one in a World Series game.

In 1938 the Cincinnati Reds were in the process of building
a team that would be a pennant winner in '39 and a world
champion in '40. They were still a year away now, but they
had on their squad a number of talented young players, among
them a wild, hard-throwing left-handed pitcher named Vander Meer. While the Reds were sure that he would in time
become an outstanding pitcher he, like the rest of the club, had
not yet lived up to his promise. Then, on June 11, he was
chosen to start against the Boston Braves. He amazed everybody, including his teammates, by pitching a no-hit game. He
walked only three men, also an astounding feat for this scatter-
armed young man, and faced only twenty-eight batters. It
was the first no-hitter pitched by a Cincinnati player since 1919
and the first one pitched in the big leagues in over a year.

The Reds began to feel that Vander Meer was on his way
to stardom. He was scheduled to pitch again four days later in
Brooklyn. This was a memorable evening in a borough noted
for its memorable events. It was the first night game in the history of Ebbets Field and young Vander Meer made certain that

no one in the park that night ever forgot it. As inning after inning passed and Johnny set down the Dodgers without a hit, a
curious change came over the crowd. The Brooklyn fans, then
known as the world's most partisan, began to cheer for the
Cincinnati pitcher. As the Reds had built up a 6-0 lead, it
seemed obvious that the game was now out of reach of the
home team. Knowing the Dodgers were going to lose, the fans
hoped to be in on an event unique in the history of baseball.
Vander Meer was nearing his second straight no-hitter.

It was a shaky performance, nonetheless. After eight innings
he had walked five Brooklyn hitters and he appeared tired as
he came out for the ninth. His first three pitches to Buddy
Hassett were wide. He got his next two pitches over the plate
and finally Hassett grounded out. Vander Meer then threw
the crowd into a frenzy by walking three hitters in a row to fill
the bases. Just as it seemed he would crack under the pressure,
he got the ball over the plate to Ernie Koy and the big Dodger
outfielder forced a runner at the plate. The last hitter was Leo
Durocher. Leo went after a fast ball and hit a fly to short
center field.

It was Vander Meer's brightest moment. He never again
was the pitcher he had been in those two games and he knew
only mediocrity for the rest of his career. But he had won a
permanent place in the legend of the sport with his unprecedented achievement. That the ungainly nickname "The Double
No-Hit Kid" is still associated with him is an added tribute to
the enduring quality of his feat.

Larsen is another pitcher who burst wholly unexpectedly
into the company of baseball's most illustrious names. This is
not to suggest that he was completely unfamiliar to fame.
Pitching for the Baltimore Orioles in 1954 he had compiled

the horrible record of three victories and twenty-one defeats, a notable performance in any league. Pitching against the Dodgers in the 1955 Series he had been soundly thrashed, but he left his mark when he came to bat early in the game and raised a high pop foul which hit the owner of the Yankees, Del Webb, squarely on the top of the head. And during spring training in 1956 he violated Casey Stengel's midnight curfew rule and smashed his car into a tree at 5:30 A.M. But, because he was quick to admit to Stengel that he was in the wrong, Casey forgave him.

"The man was either out too late or up too early," Stengel explained as he closed the case.

And Larsen was equally concise. "It was just a bad day," he told the reporters.

There had never been any doubt about Larsen's natural ability and that was why the Yankees obtained him from Baltimore after the 1954 season. They hoped that he would eventually straighten himself out and become a winning pitcher. Besides his talent he always had shown courage and coolness in adversity and never gave up without a struggle. Perhaps Jimmy Dykes, his manager at Balitmore, summed up the young man's character when he said, "The only thing Larsen fears is sleep."

Larsen got his shot at glory in the 1956 World Series. After a poor start that season he had developed the knack of delivering his pitches without a windup and his new motion helped him to considerable success during the later part of the pennant race. Stengel counted on him for heavy duty in the Series. Don started the second game against the Dodgers and looked very much like the old Larsen. Given a six-run lead, he suffered a wild spell in the second inning and Stengel had to take him out. The Yankees lost the game.

But Larsen shrugged off this disaster and was ready when Stengel called on him again. It was the toughest assignment of the Series. Each club had won two games and it was felt that the team which won the fifth game would go on to win the championship; the Yankees themselves felt that they would have to win the game because the Series then shifted to Ebbets Field and it would be difficult to have to come from behind in the Dodgers' own park. Adding to Larsen's burden was the fact that his rival pitcher was the resolute Sal Maglie.

On that day, October 8, 1956, Larsen pitched what was probably the finest game ever fashioned by a big leaguer. No one had ever pitched a no-hitter in the World Series before, and no one had pitched a perfect game in the big leagues since 1922. But Larsen, handling the Dodgers with such ease that few in the crowd appreciated the perfection of his performance, retired each of the twenty-seven batters he faced. Even more important to the Yankees was the fact that he outpitched Maglie and set the Yankees on the road to the championship. Only when there was one out left did the big crowd at Yankee Stadium seem to appreciate the magnitude of his performance; perhaps up until then they did not really believe that it was possible. With two men out in the ninth inning and the Yankees leading, 2-0, the Dodgers sent Dale Mitchell to bat as a pinch hitter. He was an experienced and dangerous batsman.

"He really scared me up there," Larsen said later. "Looking back on it, though, I know how much pressure he was under. He must have been paralyzed. That made two of us."

Larsen got two strikes over on Mitchell, then fired a fast ball across the outside corner of the plate. Mitchell cocked his bat, then did not swing. When the umpire, calling it strike three, thrust his right arm into the air it was as if he had pulled a lever which set free a torrent of tumult and shouting. Catcher Yogi Berra rushed to the mound and hurled his stubby body into Larsen's arms. The other Yankees poured from the dugout to bury their hero under an avalanche of hugs, slaps and violent handshakes. Frenzied fans tumbled out of the stands to get in their licks at the beleaguered pitcher before he disappeared down the steps of the Yankee dugout. Mitchell stood in the batter's box, making his feeble protest to a world that had suddenly lost interest in him.

It is fitting that we close our chapter with Torger Tokle. No American athlete of our time displayed more of the qualities of which we have been speaking than Tokle, and the fact that he was a naturalized citizen only emphasizes this point. The purists of the ski-jumping world looked down their noses at Torger; his form was never quite up to that of the great European jumpers. But Americans took him to their hearts, just as they had idolized Babe Ruth in spite of his frequent strike-outs and Jack Dempsey in spite of his inferiority to Gene Tunney as a boxer. Tokle, whose legs may have wobbled in flight, happened to jump farther than anybody else.

That was why the crowds gathered at Iron Mountain, Michigan, on March 1, 1942. People who didn't know how to strap on a pair of skis were interested in the jumping competition that day simply because the great Torger Tokle was to be among the jumpers. He intrigued anyone who ever saw him. For the average person the very thought of zooming down a steep incline at seventy miles an hour and then taking off into space is a frightening experience. Torger doubled the hazards by completely outjumping most of the hills on which he performed. Few American jumping towers before World War II were constructed to contain the long leaps of the European masters. If one jumped too far he overshot the landing incline and hit flat ground. The record here at Iron Mountain stood at 267 feet and the spectators were anxious to see what young Tokle could do with it.

He left little doubt in their minds the first time he went down the chute. He took off on a leap of 281 feet, far outdistancing his rivals that day and breaking the local record. His jump, it was duly noted, fell only seven feet short of the all-time American record of 288 feet which he had set the year before in the state of Washington. Loud cheers and the honking of auto horns acclaimed his feat.

But Torger had another jump left that day. He felt he could do better. The skiing conditions were perfect and there was a hard crust of snow underfoot. As he prepared for his second jump he was mildly upset, but not nearly as dismayed as the onlookers were, to discover that one of his skis was cracked. The chance of breaking a leg or a neck are considerable under any jumping conditions. To take off on a cracked ski requires fantastic courage and boundless confidence.

Tokle had both qualities in profusion. He calmly pushed off at the top of the inrun and roared down at seventy miles an hour. As he approached its end he swayed slightly from side to side to pick up even more speed. Then, timing his leap perfectly, he pushed off on those magnificent springs which he successfully disguised as his legs, bent forward almost horizontally and soared through space. A gasp came from the crowd as it became apparent that he was passing his previous record-breaking leap. Outjumping the hill by nineteen feet, he finally came back to earth on flat ground, leaning a little to one side to ease the shock on his cracked ski. For a moment he seemed to lose his balance, then came erect again and completed his remarkable jump upright. A mighty cheer came from the crowd when the jump had been measured. It was 289 feet, farther than any man had ever jumped in the Western Hemisphere.

"I had the feeling the ground was coming up to meet me," he said later.

It was the climax of Tokle's three-year jumping career in the United States, a career which had begun the day after he stepped off a boat from Norway. Born in the little Norwegian town of Lokken Verk, he was one of twenty children. Like most other Norwegians he grew up on skis. At three he was skiing, at six he was making his first jump in a field near his home and at nine he entered a local tournament and took on an eighty-foot leap.

He kept jumping as he grew up, but nobody in his native land had ever heard of him. He was just another boy in a little sulphur-mining community, and his opportunities to improve his condition were very poor. Then his older brother, Kyrre, who was working in the United States, returned home for a visit. Young Torger talked him into taking him back to America with him.

Torger landed in New York on January 21, 1939, a penniless young man of nineteen who couldn't speak a word of English. The next day he and his brother took a boat up the Hudson River to Bear Mountain, where Kyrre was to enter a ski-jumping meet. Torger, who had brought his skis, decided to enter it, too. Because he was lightly regarded, he was placed in the Class B event, then went out and amazed everybody by outjumping even the skiers in the Class A event.

Now ski enthusiasts were talking about this newcomer whose powerful legs propelled him farther than anyone else around. He was a marvel. His form was below par, not comparable to that of the few European masters who had so far been seen in the United States, and not even as good as our own better jumpers. Ski jumping is a highly complex sport in which the judges give points for form as well as distance. Torger had little grace as he took off and, in flight, he had trouble keeping his feet together. But somehow, when all the jumps had been measured, there was nobody close to Tokle.

"There'll never be another like him," John Martin, the manager of the resort at Bear Mountain where Torger did much of his jumping, said recently. "What Dempsey, Ruth and Bill Tilden were to their sports, Torger was to skiing. He gave the game the glamour that converted a weekly Norseman's outing into a Sunday spectacle that attracted 20,000 people. Millions learned that the way Torger jumped, a slip might mean death—that here was a sport taking more nerve than any other."

You could see the vitality in his body at a glance. Like most jumpers he was a short man, standing less than five feet seven and weighing about 160 pounds. But his shoulders were broad and his legs stocky and there was power in every movement he made. The crowds liked his modesty, too, and his big smile and his honest blue eyes.

"The secret is balance," he once said in answer to a question about his success. "I can't say much about it. You either have it or you don't. I guess I have it."

He certainly did. In three years of competitive jumping he broke nineteen hill records. He won forty-two of the forty-eight meets in which he jumped and in the six he failed to win he made the longest leap of the day. His victories were taken from him because the judges gave his rivals extra points for pretty form. This always annoyed American fans. They believed the sport had a sound criterion in distance; why complicate matters by making a man (whose leap hadn't come close to Tokle's) the champion chiefly because he appeared more graceful in flight?

By 1942, however, there was more on Tokle's mind than jumping. The United States was at war and Torger's own country, Norway, had been overrun by the Nazis. He felt that the time for sports had passed. He had already become an American citizen and now he tried to get in the United States Army. Turned down at first because of defective teeth, he had the trouble remedied at his own expense, and entered as a private.

He volunteered, naturally, for the ski troops. He took the war seriously indeed, never losing sight of the fact that the enemy had enslaved his own people in Norway and were threatening to do the same with those of his adopted country. When his moment came, he fought with savage courage.

It was in early March, 1945, just three years after he had set the new jump record back on Iron Mountain, that Torger came face to face with the enemy. He was T/Sgt. Tokle now, a platoon leader in the Tenth Mountain Division. His outfit was attacking the Germans in the rugged Apennine Mountains in northern Italy. As a prelude to a general offensive Torger led his platoon on an assault against an imposing ridge west of Mount Belvedere. An Associated Press story recounted the troops' exploit:

"The ridge, five miles long and 3,500 feet high, is so sheer the mountaineers had to use fixed ropes and other special peak-climbing equipment to get up its rocky sides. At the top they caught the German garrison completely by surprise, seized the entire mass and held it for three days against repeated desperate German counter-attacks. Officers of other units said the feat was one of the most brilliant mountain climbing operations of this campaign."

Tokle's outfit then began an attack on the little town of Monte Forte on March 3. "Torger was all over the place," Lyle Munson, one of his buddies, has recalled. "He plugged many a gap. A German machine gun was holding up his platoon and Torger and another guy got a bazooka and were trying to knock it out. I saw him load once. The first shell was a dud. And then, before he had a chance to reload, an 88-mm. shell plopped in on him."

Torger Tokle was only twenty-five years old when he died. Despite the sneers of the purists and the brevity of his career, his name remains the brightest in the history of American skiing. Courage was a part of him always, not simply a tool to be used on the athletic field. He died as he had lived—with dash and valor. His day in the sun was a bright one.

Chapter 16 **Conclusion**

There has been no attempt to identify all of the heroes of these pages as the greatest, or the bravest, athletes their sports have known. Neither have we suggested that only the sports included here are capable of producing men of indomitable courage and perseverance. The characters and personalities of these men vary as widely as the sports in which they compete, and some have left themselves open to criticism in respects other than their intense will to win. They share only that quality which has been the subject of our book. "Deeds cannot dream what dreams can do," the poet writes, but we like to think that the deeds recounted in our pages will continue to stir dreams in the hearts of those who believe that man has not yet pushed to the outer rim of his capacity. Ahead of us lie challenges greater than the four-minute mile. The man who knows that the race is not always to the swift, nor the battle to the strong, may reach a point beyond the assumed limits of speed and strength. He is the chief justification of America's preoccupation with spectator sports.

Set in Linotype Janson
Format by Nancy Etheredge
Manufactured by The Haddon Craftsmen, Inc.
Published by HARPER & BROTHERS, *New York*